Kindergarten

Teacher's Edition

Senior Authors J. David Cooper, John J. Pikulski

Authors Patricia A. Ackerman, Kathryn H. Au, David J. Chard, Gilbert G. Garcia, Claude N. Goldenberg, Marjorie Y. Lipson, Susan E. Page, Shane Templeton, Sheila W. Valencia, MaryEllen Vogt

Consultants Linda H. Butler, Linnea C. Ehri, Carla B. Ford

HOUGHTON MIFFLIN   BOSTON • MORRIS PLAINS, NJ

California • Colorado • Georgia • Illinois • New Jersey • Texas

Literature Reviewers

Consultants: **Dr. Adela Artola Allen**, Associate Dean, Graduate College, Associate Vice President for Inter-American Relations, University of Arizona, Tucson, Arizona; **Dr. Manley Begay**, Co-director of the Harvard Project on American Indian Economic Development, Director of the National Executive Education Program for Native Americans, Harvard University, John F. Kennedy School of Government, Cambridge, Massachusetts; **Dr. Nicholas Kannellos**, Director, Arte Publico Press, Director, Recovering the U.S. Hispanic Literacy Heritage Project, University of Houston, Texas; **Mildred Lee**, author and former head of Library Services for Sonoma County, Santa Rosa, California; **Dr. Barbara Moy**, Director of the Office of Communication Arts, Detroit Public Schools, Michigan; **Norma Naranjo**, Clark County School District, Las Vegas, Nevada; **Dr. Arlette Ingram Willis**, Associate Professor, Department of Curriculum and Instruction, Division of Language and Literacy, University of Illinois at Urbana-Champaign, Illinois

Teachers: **Helen Brooks**, Vestavia Hills Elementary School, Birmingham, Alabama; **Patricia Buchanan**, Thurgood Marshall School, Newark, Delaware; **Gail Connor**, Language Arts Resource Teacher, Duval County, Jacksonville, Florida; **Vicki DeMott**, McClean Science/Technology School, Wichita, Kansas; **Marge Egenhoffer**, Dixon Elementary School, Brookline, Wisconsin; **Mary Jew Mori**, Griffin Avenue Elementary, Los Angeles, California

Program Reviewers

Supervisors: **Judy Artz**, Middletown Monroe City School District, Ohio; **James Bennett**, Elkhart Schools, Elkhart, Indiana; **Kay Buckner-Seal**, Wayne County, Michigan; **Charlotte Carr**, Seattle School District, Washington; **Sister Marion Christi**, St. Matthews School, Archdiocese of Philadelphia, Pennsylvania; **Alvina Crouse**, Garden Place Elementary, Denver Public Schools, Colorado; **Peggy DeLapp**, Minneapolis, Minnesota; **Carol Erlandson**, Wayne Township Schools, Marion County, Indianapolis; **Brenda Feeney**, North Kansas City School District, Missouri; **Winnie Huebsch**, Sheboygan Area Schools, Wisconsin; **Brenda Mickey**, Winston-Salem/Forsyth County Schools, North Carolina; **Audrey Miller**, Sharpe Elementary School, Camden, New Jersey; **JoAnne Piccolo**, Rocky Mountain Elementary, Adams 12 District, Colorado; **Sarah Rentz**, East Baton Rouge Parish School District, Louisiana; **Kathy Sullivan**, Omaha Public Schools, Nebraska; **Rosie Washington**, Kuny Elementary, Gary, Indiana; **Theresa Wishart**, Knox County Public Schools, Tennessee

Teachers: **Carol Brockhouse**, Madison Schools, Wayne Westland Schools, Michigan; **Eva Jean Conway**, R.C. Hill School, Valley View School District, Illinois; **Carol Daley**, Jane Addams School, Sioux Falls, South Dakota; **Karen Landers**, Watwood Elementary, Talladega County, Alabama; **Barb LeFerrier**, Mullenix Ridge Elementary, South Kitsap District, Port Orchard, Washington; **Loretta Piggee**, Nobel School, Gary, Indiana; **Cheryl Remash**, Webster Elementary School, Manchester, New Hampshire; **Marilynn Rose**, Michigan; **Kathy Scholtz**, Amesbury Elementary School, Amesbury, Massachusetts; **Dottie Thompson**, Erwin Elementary, Jefferson County, Alabama; **Dana Vassar**, Moore Elementary School, Winston-Salem, North Carolina; **Joy Walls**, Ibraham Elementary School, Winston-Salem, North Carolina; **Elaine Warwick**, Fairview Elementary, Williamson County, Tennessee

Credits

Cover and Theme Opener
Don Stuart

Assignment Photography
Joel Benjamin
pp. T9, T11, T13, T21, T23, T43, T53, T67, T75, T97, T121, T129, T147

Parker/Boon Productions
p. T53

Illustration
Nathan Y. Jarvis
p. T79

Alexi Natchev
p. T119

Acknowledgments

Grateful acknowledgment is made for permission to reprint copyrighted material as follows:

Theme 5
Feast for Ten, by Cathryn Falwell. Copyright © 1993 by Cathryn Falwell. Reprinted by arrangement with Houghton Mifflin Company.

Theme 5

Let's Count!

OBJECTIVES

Phonemic Awareness blending onset and rime; words in oral sentences

Phonics sounds for letters *P, p; G, g; F, f*

Decoding *-an* word family

High-Frequency Words recognize two new high-frequency words

Reading Strategies monitor/clarify; summarize; question; phonics/decoding

Comprehension Skills categorize and classify; story structure: beginning, middle, end

Vocabulary describing words; number words; rhyming words; naming words

Writing list; journals; number rhyme; silly poem; friendly letter; describing words

Listening/Speaking/Viewing activities to support vocabulary expansion and writing

Let's Count!
Literature Resources

Teacher Read Aloud
Benny's Pennies
fiction by Pat Brisson
pages T10–T11

Big Book
Feast for 10
concepts book by Cathryn Falwell
pages T18–T19, T28–T33

Math Link
What's on the Menu?
nonfiction
pages T40–T41

Decodable Phonics Library
Nat, Pat, and Nan
page T35

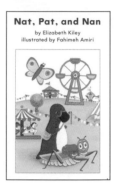

Nat, Pat, and Nan
by Elizabeth Kiley
illustrated by Fahimeh Amiri

Teacher Read Aloud
Counting Noodles
a traditional tale
pages T62–T65

Big Book
Ten Little Puppies
a traditional counting song adapted by Elena Vázquez
pages T72–T73, T82–T87

Art Link
Meet Scott Nash
nonfiction
pages T94–T95

Decodable Phonics Library
Go, Cat!
page T89

Go, Cat
by Elizabeth Kiley
illustrated by Nancy Speir

Teacher Read Aloud
Peace and Quiet
a Russian folktale
pages T116–T119

Revisit the Big Books:
Feast for 10
pages 126–127

Ten Little Puppies
pages 136–137

Revisit the Links: Math
What's on the Menu?
page T144

Art
Meet Scott Nash
page T145

Decodable Phonics Library
Pat and Nan
page T139

Pat and Nan
by Elizabeth Kiley
illustrated by Penny Carter

Big Books for Use All Year

**From Apples
to Zebras:
A Book of ABC's**

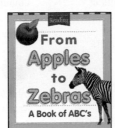

**Higglety Pigglety:
A Book of Rhymes**

Leveled Books

See Cumulative Listing of Leveled Books.

Phonics Library

Decodable

· Nat, Pat, and Nan

· Go, Cat!

· Pat and Nan

Lessons, pages
T35, T89, T139

On My Way Practice Reader

Easy | On Level

Nan Can!
by Demaris Tyler
page T153

Little Big Books

On Level | Challenge

Feast for 10

**Ten Little
Puppies**

 Audiotape
Let's Count!

**Houghton Mifflin
Classroom Bookshelf**
Level K

**Little Readers
for Guided Reading**
Collection K

Bibliography

Books for Browsing

 **Animal 123's**
by The World Wildlife Fund
Cedco 1998 (40p)
Colorful photographs show wild animals, from one owl to twenty lions.

 Splash!
by Ann Jonas
Greenwillow 1995 (24p)
A girl and a menagerie of animals swim, fall in, and climb out of a pond in changing combinations.

One Hole in the Road
by W. Nikola-Lisa
Holt 1996 (32p)
Passers-by watch as ten workmen scurry to fix one hole in the road.

Three Little Kittens *
by Paul Galdone
Clarion 1986 (32p) also paper
Three kittens lose their mittens in this favorite Mother Goose rhyme.

More, Fewer, Less
by Tana Hoban
Greenwillow 1998 (32p)
Photos show groupings of objects like shells, vegetables, and sheep in larger and smaller numbers.

Dear Daisy, Get Well Soon
by Maggie Smith
Crown 2000 (40p)
When Daisy comes down with the chicken pox, Peter proves he's a friend she can count on.

 Let's Count
by Tana Hoban
Greenwillow 1999 (32p)
Photographs of every-day objects introduce the numbers from one to one hundred.

Ten Rosy Roses
by Eve Merriam
Harper 1999 (32p)
One by one, a group of children pick ten roses for their teacher in this counting rhyme.

 Every Buddy Counts
by Stuart Murphy
Harper 1997 (32p)
also paper
A girl counts all her pals, including one hamster, five neighbors, and ten teddy bears.

Books for Teacher Read Aloud

Can You Top That?
by W. Nikola-Lisa
Lee & Low 2000 (32p)
A group of children try to outdo each other imagining increasing numbers of fantastic animals.

Millions of Cats
by Wanda Gag
Putnam 1996 (32p) paper
An old man who sets off to find one kitten returns home with oodles of cats. Available in Spanish as *Millones de gatos*.

Rooster's Off to See the World
by Eric Carle
Simon 1972 (32p) also paper
Off to see the world, Rooster is joined by fourteen animals along the way.

Emily's First 100 Days of School
by Rosemary Wells
Hyperion 2000 (64p)
Counting each day from 1 to 100, Emily and her classmates learn numbers in many different ways.

Ten Apples Up On Top
by Dr. Seuss
Random 1961 (64p)
A lion, a tiger, and a dog try to outdo each other balancing apples on their heads.

Night Lights
by Steven Schnur
Farrar 2000 (32p)
Before she goes to bed, Melinda counts the lights around her, from night lights to stars.

How Many Stars in the Sky?
by Lenny Hort
Tambourine 1991 (32p) also paper
Unable to sleep, a father and son look for a good place to count the stars in the sky.

Quack and Count
by Keith Baker
Harcourt 1999 (32p)
Playful ducklings demonstrate the many ways to count to seven in this rhyming look at addition.

123 Moose
by Andrea Helman & Art Wolfe
Sasquatch (32p) 1998
Photographs and text present the wildlife of the Pacific Northwest in this counting book.

Emeka's Gift
by Ifeoma Onyefulu
Cobblehill 1995 (32p)
A Nigerian boy counts objects at a market.

* = Included in Houghton Mifflin Classroom Bookshelf, Level K

Key

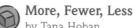 **Science**

Social Studies

Multicultural

Music

Math

Classic

Art

Books for Shared Reading

 Somewhere in the Ocean
by Jennifer Ward and T. J. Marsh
Rising Moon 2000 (32p)
A counting song modeled after "Over in the Meadow" presents sea animals and their offspring.

 A Tree for Me
by Nancy Van Laan
Knopf 2000 (32p)
A child climbs five trees and discovers them occupied by animals, from one owl to five spiders.

 Can You Count Ten Toes?*
by Lezlie Evans
Houghton 1999 (32p)
Rhyming text invites readers to count to ten in languages including Spanish, Korean, and Zulu.

 Five Little Monkeys Jumping on the Bed
by Eileen Christelow
Clarion 1989 (32p) also paper
Five mischievous monkeys bouncing on a bed fall off and bump their heads. See others in series.

 One Duck Stuck
by Phyllis Root
Candlewick 1998 (32p)
An increasing number of animals try to help a duck stuck in a mucky marsh.

 Over in the Meadow
by John Langstaff
Harcourt 1957 (32p) also paper
A Caldecott Honor book, this traditional rhyme counts animals and their babies.

 Roll Over! A Counting Song*
by Merle Peek
Clarion 1981 (32p) also paper
One by one, a boy's nine animal friends roll over and fall out of his bed in this song.

Books for Phonics Read Aloud

 Five Little Ducks
by Pamela Paparone
North-South 1995 (32p)
Mother Duck sets out to find her disappearing duckling in this traditional rhyme. Available in Spanish as *Los cinco patitos.*

 Ten Flashing Fireflies
by Philomen Sturges
North-South 1995 (32p)
A girl and boy count up to ten and down again as they catch and then release ten fireflies.

 Ten Clean Pigs/ Ten Dirty Pigs
by Carol Roth
North-South 1999 (32p)
Ten pigs have fun getting clean and then getting dirty again.

From Head to Toe
by Eric Carle
Harper 1997 (32p)
With the words "Can you do it?" animals invite children to imitate their movement.

* = Included in Houghton Mifflin Classroom Bookshelf, Level K

Theme 5

Theme at a Glance

Theme Concept: *Numbers are important to us in many ways.*

✅ **Indicates Tested Skills**

Learning to Read

	Phonemic Awareness and Phonics	High-Frequency Words	Comprehension Skills and Strategies
WEEK 1 **Read Aloud** **Benny's Pennies** **Big Book** **Feast for 10** **Math Link** **What's on the Menu?** **Phonics Library** *"Nat, Pat, and Nan"* 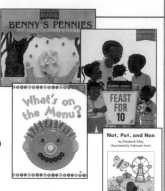	✅ Phonemic Awareness: Blending Onset and Rime, *T9, T17, T27, T39, T47* ✅ Initial Consonant *p, T12–T13, T20–T21* ✅ Blending *-an* words, *T34, T42–T43* **Phonics/Decoding** Review: Familiar Consonants; *-an, -at* words, *T13, T20, T36, T44, T50, T52*	✅ High-Frequency Words, *T22–T23, T35, T51* **Word Wall** *T8, T16, T26, T38, T46*	✅ Comprehension: Categorize and Classify, *T10, T18, T29, T31, T40, T48* **Strategies:** Monitor/Clarify, *T10, T18, T29, T30, T32, T40* Phonics/Decoding, *T35*
WEEK 2 **Read Aloud** **Counting Noodles** **Big Book** **Ten Little Puppies** **Art Link** **Meet Scott Nash** **Phonics Library** *"Go, Cat!"* 	✅ Phonemic Awareness: Blending Onset and Rime, *T61, T71, T81, T93, T101* ✅ Initial Consonant *g, T66–T67, T74–T75* ✅ Blending *-an* words, *T88, T96–T97* **Phonics/Decoding** Review: Familiar Consonants; *-an, -at* words, *T67, T74, T90, T98, T104, T106*	✅ High-Frequency Words, *T76–T77, T89, T105* **Word Wall** *T60, T70, T80, T92, T100*	✅ Comprehension: Story Structure: Beginning, Middle, End, *T62, T72, T83, T85, T102* **Strategies:** Summarize, *T62, T72, T83, T85, T94* Phonics/Decoding, *T89*
WEEK 3 **Read Aloud** **Peace and Quiet** **Big Book** **Feast for 10** **Ten Little Puppies** **Math and Art Links** **What's on the Menu?** **Meet Scott Nash** **Phonics Library** *"Pat and Nan"* 	✅ Phonemic Awareness: Blending Onset and Rime, *T115, T125, T135, T143, T151* ✅ Word in Oral Sentences, *T115, T125, T135, T143, T151* ✅ Initial Consonant *f, T120–T121, T128–T129* ✅ Blending *-an* words, *T138, T146–T147* **Phonics/Decoding** Review: Familiar Consonants; *-an, -at* words, *T121, T128, T140, T148, T154, T156*	High-Frequency Words, *T130–T131, T139, T155* **Word Wall** *T114, T124, T134, T142, T150*	✅ Comprehension: Story Structure: Beginning, Middle, End, *T116, T137, T152* Categorize and Classify, *T126, T127, T144, T145, T152* **Strategies:** Question, *T116, T126, T136* Monitor/Clarify, *T144, T145* Phonics/Decoding, *T139*

Pacing	Multi–age Classroom	Technology 
• This theme is designed to take approximately 3 weeks, depending on your students' needs.	**Related theme—:** • **Grade 1:** *Surprise!*	**Education Place: www.eduplace.com** Log on to Education Place for more activities relating to *Let's Count!* **Lesson Planner CD-ROM:** Customize your planning for *Let's Count!* with the Lesson Planner.

Word Work		Writing & Language			Centers
High-Frequency Word Practice	**Building Words**	**Oral Language**	**Writing**	**Listening/ Speaking/Viewing**	**Content Areas**
Matching Words, *T14* Building Sentences, *T24*	Word Family *-an, T36* Word Families *-at, -an, T44, T52*	**Using Describing Words** • describing objects by number and color, *T15* **Vocabulary Expansion** • using number words, *T25*	**Shared Writing** • writing a list, *T37* **Interactive Writing** • writing a list, *T45* **Independent Writing** • Journals, *T53*	Listening, Viewing, and Speaking, *T15* Viewing and Speaking, *T45*	Book Center, *T11* Phonics Center, *T13, T21, T43* Writing Center, *T15, T45* Science Center, *T19* Art Center, *T25, T33*
Matching Words, *T68* Building Sentences, *T78*	Word Family *-an, T90* Word Families *-at, -an, T98* Word Families *-at, -an, T106*	**Rhyming Words** • rhyming pairs, *T69* **Vocabulary Expansion** • using naming words, *T79*	**Shared Writing** • a number rhyme, *T91* **Interactive Writing** • writing a poem, *T99* **Independent Writing** • Journals, *T107*	Listening and Speaking, *T69, T79*	Book Center, *T63, T107* Phonics Center, *T67, T75, T97* Writing Center, *T69, T99* Dramatic Play Center, *T63* Math Center, *T73, T87* Art Center, *T79, T86*
Matching Words, *T122* Building Sentences, *T132*	Word Family *-an, T140* Word Families *-an, -at, T148, T156*	**Using Describing Words** • describing words, *T123* **Vocabulary Expansion** • describing food, *T133*	**Shared Writing** • writing a friendly letter, *T141* **Interactive Writing** • using describing words, *T149* **Independent Writing** • Journals, *T157*	Speaking, *T123, T141* Viewing and Speaking, *T133*	Book Center, *T117* Phonics Center, *T121, T129, T147* Writing Center, *T123, T149* Art Center, *T127, T137, T145* Science Center, *T133*

Planning for Assessment

Use these resources to meet your assessment needs. For additional information, see the *Teacher's Assessment Handbook*.

Emerging Literacy Survey

Technology
**Lexia CD-ROM
Quick Phonics Assessemnt**

Diagnostic Planning

Emerging Literacy Survey

- If you have used this survey to obtain baseline data on the skills children brought with them to kindergarten, this might be a good time to re-administer all or parts of the survey to chart progress, to identify areas of strength and need, and to test the need for early intervention.

Lexia Quick Phonics Assessment CD-ROM

- Can be used to identify students who need more help with phonics.

Ongoing Assessment

Phonemic Awareness:
- **Practice Book,** pp. 135–136, 145–146, 155–156

Phonics:
- **Practice Book,** pp. 137, 140–141, 147, 150–151, 158, 160–161

Comprehension:
- Reading Responses **Practice Book,** pp. 133–134, 139, 143–144, 149, 153–154, 157

Writing:
- Writing samples for portfolio

Informal Assessment:
- **Diagnotics Checks,** pp. T23, T33, T51, T77, T86, T97, T105, T131, T147, T155

Integrated Theme Test

Theme Skills Test

End-of-Theme Assessment

Integrated Theme Test:
- Assesses children's progress as readers and writers in a format that reflects instruction. Simple decodable texts test reading skills in context.

Theme Skills Test:
- Assesses children's mastery of specific reading and language arts skills taught in the theme.

Kindergarten Benchmarks

For your planning, listed here are the instructional goals and activities that help develop benchmark behaviors for kindergartners. Use this list to plan instruction and to monitor children's progress. See the Checklist of skills found on TE p. T159.

Theme Lessons and Actvities:	Benchmark Behaviors:
Oral Language	
• songs, rhymes, chants, fingerplays • shared reading	• can listen to story attentively • can participate in the shared reading experience
Phonemic Awareness	
• blending and segmenting onset and rime • words in oral sentences • beginning sounds	• can blend sounds into meaningful units
Phonics	
• initial consonants *p, g, f* • word family *-an*	• can name single letters and their sounds • can decode some common CVC words
Concepts of Print	
• distinguish letter/word/sentence • first/last letter in a written word	• can recognize common print conventions
Reading	
• decodable texts • high-frequency words *and, go*	• can read and write a few words • can select a letter to represent a sound
Comprehension	
• categorize and classify • story structure	• can think critically about a text • can use effective reading strategies
Writing and Language	
• writing simple phrases or sentences • using describing words	• can label pictures using phonetic spellings • can write independently

Theme 5

Launching the Theme

Let's Count!

> Quack! Quack! Quack!
>
> Five little ducks that I once knew,
> Big ones, little ones, skinny ones too,
> But the one little duck
>   with a feather on his back,
> He led the others with a
>   "Quack! Quack! Quack!"
>
> a Traditional Song

Theme Poster: Let's Count!

▶ Using the Theme Poster

Read the rhyme aloud. Children chime in when they're ready. Emphasize the rhythm with a clap or a stomp. Use rhythm instruments just for fun! Children can march to "Quack! Quack! Quack!"

- Together count the ducks on the poster. Have volunteers point out the big, little, and skinny ducks, as well as the duck leader.
- Hang the poster in the classroom and recite the rhyme during transitions.
- Use the poster throughout the theme as a springboard for number activities.

■ **Week 1** After reading *Benny's Pennies,* children can count out 5 pennies and write a class story about buying 5 ducks.

■ **Week 2** Write a rhyme about 5 little puppies.

■ **Week 3** After rereading *Feast for 10,* have groups of children plan, illustrate, and label a feast for ducks.

MULTI-AGE Classroom

Related Theme:

Grade 1 . . . Surprise!

Grade K . . . Let's Count!

▶ Theme Poem: "One, Two, Three, Four, Five"

Read the poem aloud. Have children echo-read it. When it is familiar, cover the number words with self-sticks notes and ask volunteers to write the numerals. Then read the poem *with* the numbers. Reinforce that the words and the numerals have the same meaning.

One, Two, Three, Four, Five

One, two, three, four, five,
Once I caught a fish alive!
Six, seven, eight, nine, ten,
Then I let it go again.
Why did you let it go?
Because it bit my finger so.
Which of your fingers did it bite?
This little finger on the right.

a Mother Goose Rhyme

Higglety Pigglety: A Book of Rhymes, **page 22**

On-Going Project

Materials • paper • markers • yarn

Class Counting Book Read lots of counting books aloud throughout the theme. Discuss what is the same about them and what makes each one unique. Then tell children they'll be authors and illustrators for a Class Counting Book. Decide together how the book will be   a page or two for each number, 1 to 10 or higher. Children write the numeral for each page, decide upon the illustrations, design the cover, and bind the book in the Art Center. Laminated pages make a sturdy book that can be shelved in the Class or School Library for children to enjoy time and again.

Challenge Some children who are able might make a "1 to 10 and Back Again" book. This book counts up to 10 and back to 1 again.

www.eduplace.com
Log onto *Education Place* for more activities relating to *Let's Count!*

Lesson Planner CD-ROM
Customize your planning for *Let's Count!* with the Lesson Planner.

Book Adventure
www.bookadventure.org
This Internet reading-incentive program provides thousands of titles for students to read.

Home Connection

Send home the theme newsletter for *Let's Count!* to introduce the theme and suggest home activities (**Blackline Master 74**).

For other suggestions relating to *Let's Count!* see **Home/Community Connections.**

Classroom Routines

Let's Count!

To introduce a routine...

1. Demonstrate the routine for the class.
2. Cycle every child through the routine at least once with supervision.
3. Establish ground rules for acceptable work products.
4. Check children's work.
5. Praise children's growing independence.

Instructional Routines

FOUR SQUARE SOUNDS

Materials • paper, folded into four squares • crayons

Have children fold a piece of paper into four squares. Tell them that you'll say a word in parts, and they'll put the sounds together to make a word. Then they draw a picture in one square.
Blend the sounds aloud. What is the word?
Draw a picture of the word. Use CVC words that are easily drawn, such as: *cat, bug, hen, pig, rug, sun, pan, can, van,* and *fan.*

"I SEE" GUESSING GAME

Review that describing words tell how something looks or tell how many.

- Tell children that they'll play a guessing game called "I See." Explain that you'll use numbers and colors to describe something in the room. Children guess the object(s). ***I see one brown* _____.**

- Write children's responses on chart paper.

- Provide a few examples before calling on volunteers to continue the game by describing something they see.

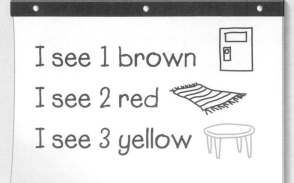

Management Routine
LINE UP

Create number cards and place them in a box labeled "Time to Line Up!" When it is time for Music class or for an assembly, tell children that it is Time to Line Up! Have each child take a card from the box and ask, "Who has 1? Who has 2?" As children line up in numerical order, they add to their knowledge of numbers. (Be sure to make enough number cards so that each child has a card.)

Teacher's Note

If children have difficulty remembering the sequence of numbers, have partners use counting mats to reinforce the correct numerical order.

Literature for Week 1
Different texts for different purposes

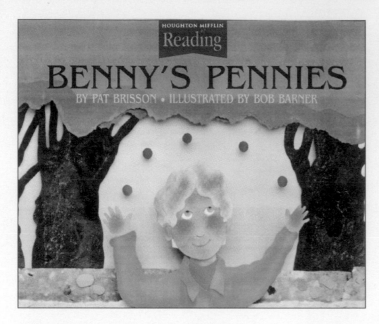

Teacher Read Aloud

Purposes

- oral language
- listening strategy
- comprehension skill

Big Books:

Higglety Pigglety: A Book of Rhymes

Purposes

- oral language development
- phonemic awareness

From Apples to Zebras: A Book of ABC's

Purposes

- alphabet recognition
- letters and sounds

Big Book: Main Selection

Purposes

- concepts of print
- reading strategy
- story language
- comprehension skills

Awards

- ★ Best Books for Children
- ★ Bank Street College Best Children's Books of the Year

Also available in Little Big Book and audiotape

Leveled Books

Math Link

31

Also in the Big Book:
– Math Link

Purposes

- reading strategies
- comprehension skills
- concepts of print

Phonics Library

Also available in Take-Home version

Purpose

- applying phonics skills and high-frequency words

On My Way Paperback

Nan Can!
by Demaris Tyler
page T153

Little Readers for Guided Reading
Collection K

Houghton Mifflin Classroom Bookshelf
Level K

Technology

www.eduplace.com

Log on to *Education Place* for more activities relating to *Let's Count!*

www.bookadventure.org

This free Internet reading incentive program provides thousands of titles for students to read.

Suggested Daily Routines

Instructional Goals

| Day 1 | Day 2 |

Learning to Read

- ✓ *Phonemic Awareness:* Blending Onset and Rime

Strategy Focus: Monitor/Clarify

- ✓ *Comprehension Skill:* Categorize and Classify

- ✓ *Phonics Skills*

Phonemic Awareness: Beginning Sound /p/ Initial Consonant *P, p;* Short *a + n*

Compare and Review: Initial Consonants: *n, c*

- ✓ *High-Frequency Word: and*

- ✓ *Concepts of Print:* Letter/Word, First/Last Letter in a Word

Day 1

Opening Routines, *T8–T9*

Word Wall
- **Phonemic Awareness:** Blending Onset and Rime

Teacher Read Aloud
Benny's Pennies, *T10–T11*
- **Strategy:** Monitor/Clarify
- **Comprehension:** Categorize and Classify

Phonics
Instruction
- Phonemic Awareness, Beginning Sound /p/, *T12–T13; Practice Book, 135–136*

Day 2

Opening Routines, *T16–T17*

Word Wall
- **Phonemic Awareness:** Blending Onset and Rime

Sharing the Big Book
Feast for 10, T18–T19
- **Strategy:** Monitor/Clarify
- **Comprehension:** Categorize and Classify

Phonics
Instruction, Practice
- Initial Consonant *p, T20–T21*
- *Practice Book, 137*

High-Frequency Word
- New Word: *and, T22–T23*
- *Practice Book, 138*

Word Work

High-Frequency Word Practice: Word Families: *-an, -at*

Day 1

High-Frequency Word Practice
- Words: *I, see, my, a, T14*

Day 2

High-Frequency Word Practice
- Building Sentences, *T24*

Writing & Language

Vocabulary Skills: Describing Words, Number Words

Writing Skills: Writing Lists, Journals

Day 1

Oral Language
- Using Describing Words, *T15*
- Listening, Speaking, and Viewing, *T15*

Day 2

Vocabulary Expansion
- Using Number Words, *T25*

✓ = tested skills

Leveled Books

Have children read in appropriate levels daily.

Phonics Library
On My Way Practice Readers
Little Big Books
Houghton Mifflin Classroom Bookshelf

Managing Small Groups
Teacher-Led Group
- Reread familiar **Phonics Library** selections

Independent Groups
- Finish *Practice Book, 133–136*
- **Phonics Center:** Theme 5, Week 1, Day 1
- Book, other Centers

Managing Small Groups
Teacher-Led Group
- Begin *Practice Book, 137–138* and handwriting **Blackline Masters 172 or 198**

Independent Groups
- Finish *Practice Book, 137–138* and handwriting **Blackline Masters 172 or 198**
- **Phonics Center:** Theme 5, Week 1, Day 2
- Science, Art, other Centers

Technology

Lesson Planner CD-ROM: Customize your planning for *Let's Count!* with the Lesson Planner.

Day 3

Opening Routines, *T26–T27*

- **Phonemic Awareness:** Blending Onset and Rime

Sharing the Big Book
Feast for 10, T28–T32
- **Strategy:** Monitor/Clarify
- **Comprehension:** Categorize and Classify, *T31; Practice Book, 139*
- **Concepts of Print:** Letter/Word, *T30;* First/Last Letter in a Word, *T32*

Phonics
Practice, Application
- Consonant *p, T34–T35*

Instruction
- Blending *-at, T34–T35; Practice Book, 140*
- **Phonics Library:** "Nat, Pat, and Nan," *T35*

Building Words
- Word Family: *-an, T36*

Shared Writing
- Writing a List, *T37*

Managing Small Groups
Teacher-Led Group
- Read **Phonics Library** sel. "Nat, Pat, and Nan"
- Write letters *A, a;* begin **Blackline Masters 157 or 183**
- Begin *Practice Book, 139–140*

Independent Groups
- Finish **Blackline Masters 157 or 183** and *Practice Book, 139–140*
- Art, other Centers

Day 4

Opening Routines, *T38–T39*

- **Phonemic Awareness:** Blending Onset and Rime

Sharing the Big Book
Math Link: "What's on the Menu," *T40–T41*
- **Strategy:** Monitor/Clarify
- **Comprehension:** Categorize and Classify
- **Concepts of Print:** Letter/Word; First/Last Letter in a Word

Phonics
Practice
- Blending *-an* Words, *T42–T43; Practice Book, 141*

Building Words
- Word Families: *-an, -at, T44*

Interactive Writing
- Writing a List, *T45*
- Viewing and Speaking, *T45*

Managing Small Groups
Teacher-Led Group
- Reread **Phonics Library** selection "Nat, Pat, and Nan"
- Begin *Practice Book, 141*

Independent Groups
- Finish *Practice Book, 141*
- **Phonics Center:** Theme 5, Week 1, Day 4
- Writing, other Centers

Day 5

Opening Routines, *T46–T47*

- **Phonemic Awareness:** Blending Onset and Rime

Revisiting the Literature
Comprehension: Categorize and Classify, *T48*

Building Fluency
- **Phonics Library:** "Nat, Pat, and Nan," *T49*

Phonics
Phonics Review
- Familiar Consonants; Word Families: *-an, -at, T50*

High-Frequency Word Review
- Words: *I, see, my, like, a, to, and, T51; Practice Book, 142*

Building Words
- Word Families: *-an, -at, T52*

Independent Writing
- Journals: Writing Lists, *T53*

Managing Small Groups
Teacher-Led Group
- Reread familiar **Phonics Library** selections
- Begin *Practice Book, 142,* **Blackline Master 36**

Independent Groups
- Reread **Phonics Library** selections
- Finish *Practice Book, 142,* **Blackline Master 36**
- Centers

Setting up the Centers

Management Tip Ask families to send in magazines and grocery store circulars for the Science Center activity on page T19.

Phonics Center

Materials • Phonics Center materials for Theme 5, Week 1

Pairs work together to sort Picture Cards by initial sound and to build words using this week's letter, *p*, and the word family *-an*. Cut the letter grids apart and put them into plastic bags, according to color. Put out the Workmats and open the Direction Chart to the appropriate day. See pages T13, T21, and T43 for this week's Phonics Center Activities.

Book Center

Materials • counting and number picture books

Fill your Book Center with number and counting books. See page T11 for this week's Book Center activity.

Ten Apples Up on Top by Dr. Suess

Animal 123's by the World Wildlife Fund

Rooster's Off to See the World by Eric Carle

Let's Count by Tana Hoban

Writing Center

Materials • chart paper

Children write and illustrate a descriptive sentence from the "I See" game. Children also write and illustrate their own grocery lists. See pages T15 and T45 for this week's Writing Center activities.

I   see   3   [   ]   [tables]   .

Science Center

Materials • five shoe boxes • food magazines and grocery store circulars • scissors

Children learn about the five food groups as they cut out and sort food pictures. See page T19 for this week's Science Center activity.

Art Center

Materials • paper plates • magazines and grocery store circulars • scissors

Children use their number skills as they write the number words and draw pictures to illustrate the numerals 1 through 5. Children also plan a feast, as in *Feast for 10*, by pasting pictures of food on paper plates. See pages T25 and T33 for this week's Art Center activities.

Learning to Read

Day 1

Day at a Glance

Learning to Read

Read Aloud:

Benny's Pennies

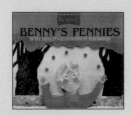

☑ **Learning About / p /,** page T12

Word Work

☑ **High-Frequency Word Practice,** page T14

Writing & Language

Oral Language, page T15

 Half-Day Kindergarten

☑ Indicates lessons for tested skills. Choose additional activities as time allows.

Opening

Calendar

Sunday	Monday	Tuesday	Wednesday	Thursday	Friday	Saturday
			1	2	3	4
5	6	7	8	9	10	11
12	13	14	15	16	17	18
19	20	21	22	23	24	25
26	27	28	29	30	31	

Count the number of days that have passed in the month so far. Ask questions to provide practice with counting and number words: *How many more days until Wednesday? Until Friday? How many days until vacation?*

Daily Message

Modeled Writing Celebrate starting a new reading theme by including the theme title in your daily message as shown in the example. Discuss with children things they may count during the theme.

> Today we start a new theme called Let's Count.

Have children chant the spelling of each word on the wall today: **I** *spells* **I** *and* **s-e-e** *spells* **see** *and* **m-y** *spells* **my** *and* **l-i-k-e** *spells* **like**.

✓ Daily Phonemic Awareness

Blending Onset and Rime

- Read the counting rhyme "One, Two, Three, Four, Five" on page 22 of *Higglety Pigglety*. Invite children to perform hand actions as you read the rhyme again.

- Play a guessing game. *I'll say some sounds. Put them together to make words from the poem:* / f /.../ ive / (five); / f /.../ ish / (fish); / b /.../ it / (bit).

- Continue as needed with more words: *sit, for, ten, bat, net, win, fan, hot, fat, not.*

- Continue by having partners confer on a word, breaking it into the beginning sound and the rest of the word. They can ask the class to blend the sounds.

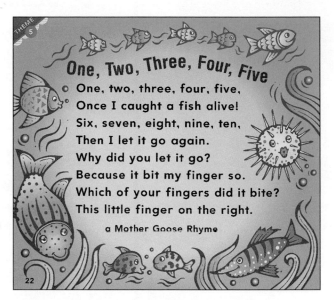

One, Two, Three, Four, Five

One, two, three, four, five,
Once I caught a fish alive!
Six, seven, eight, nine, ten,
Then I let it go again.
Why did you let it go?
Because it bit my finger so.
Which of your fingers did it bite?
This little finger on the right.

a Mother Goose Rhyme

Higglety Pigglety: A Book of Rhymes, page 22

Getting Ready to Learn

To help plan their day, tell children that they will

- listen to a story called *Benny's Pennies.*

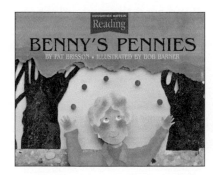

- meet a new Alphafriend, Pippa Pig.

- read, write, and explore more about numbers and number words in the Book Center.

Day 1

Read Aloud

HOUGHTON MIFFLIN
Reading

BENNY'S PENNIES
BY PAT BRISSON • ILLUSTRATED BY BOB BARNER

Purposes • oral language • listening strategy
• comprehension skill

Selection Summary
With the help of generous neighbors, a young boy thoughtfully uses his five new pennies to buy gifts.

Key Concept
money

English Language Learners

You may want to paraphrase the title as *the pennies that Benny has*. Call attention to the rhyming sounds of Benny's pennies. Make sure children know what five bright new pennies look like. As you read, point to the rhyming words. Then read the line again and have children say it with you as you point to the words.

Teacher Read Aloud
Oral Language/Comprehension

▶ **Building Background**

Display *Benny's Pennies.* Read aloud the title and the names of the author and illustrator. Point to the pennies on the cover and count them with children. Have children tell what a penny is. Ask what they would do if they had five pennies.

Strategy: Monitor/Clarify

Teacher Modeling Explain that good readers stop once in a while to make sure they understand what they are reading. Display the book as you model the Monitor/Clarify strategy.

Think Aloud

I was confused when I first read the title. The pennies on the cover didn't look like the pennies I know. So I started to read to find out what these pennies were.

Do you know what I found out? I found out that Benny wants to buy something with his pennies. Since I know people use money to buy things, I know that Benny's pennies are a kind of money.

 ### Comprehension: Categorize and Classify

Teacher Modeling Display pages 2 and 3 and read them aloud. Discuss the suggestions Benny's family makes.

Think Aloud

As I read, I'll look for things that fit into the groups that Benny's family names. I will read to see if Benny buys something beautiful, something to eat, and something to wear.

▶ Listening to the Story

Read the story aloud, slightly emphasizing the adjectives that will help children group the items purchased. Stop several times and say, *This is making sense to me. I see what Benny is doing with his pennies.*

▶ Responding

Summarizing the Story Help children summarize the story.

■ *What did Benny buy that was beautiful? What did he buy that was good to eat? What did he buy that was something to wear?*

■ *Do you think Benny had good ideas for gifts?*

Practice Book page 134 Children will complete the page at small group time.

At Group Time
Book Center

Fill your Book Center with counting books and other books about counting. Include such favorites as *Ten Apples Up on Top* by Dr. Seuss, *Let's Count* by Tana Hoban, *Rooster's Off to See the World* by Eric Carle, *Five Little Monkeys Jumping on the Bed* by Eileen Christelow, and *Animal 123's* by the World Wildlife Fund. Children can browse through the books and count the different items in the pictures.

Practice Book p. 134

Name _____

THEME 5: Let's Count!
Week One *Benny's Pennies*
Responding

134

Children
1. draw things they would buy members of their own families and the pennies it might take to buy each
2. draw things they would buy for a friend and the pennies it might take to buy each

Home Connection
Can you help me think of some good gifts for our family?

📎 Teacher's Note

● Create a chart In the Writing Center for the numerals 1 to 5. For each numeral also show a dot representation and the number name, for example: **2, · ·, two**. This will help children who want to use numerals or number names when they write.

Day 1

OBJECTIVES

Children

• identify pictures whose names begin with /p/

MATERIALS

• **Alphafriend Cards** *Pippa Pig, Nyle Noodle, Callie Cat*

• **Alphafriend Audiotape** Theme 5

• **Alphafolder** *Pippa Pig*

• **Picture Cards** *can, cot, cow, net, nine, nurse, peach, pot, purse*

• **Phonics Center:** Theme 5, Week 1, Day 1

Home Connection

A take-home version of the Alphafolder for Pippa Pig's song is on an Alphafriends **Blackline Master.** Children can share the song with their families.

Phonemic Awareness

☑ Beginning Sound

▶ Introducing the Alphafriend: Pippa Pig

Use the Alphafriend routine to introduce Pippa Pig.

1 Alphafriend Riddle Read these clues:

■ *Our new Alphafriend's sound is /p/. Say it with me: /p/.*

■ *This pudgy animal lives on a farm. She likes to play in mud puddles.*

■ *She has pink skin and oinks.*

When most hands are up, call on children until they guess *pig*.

2 Pocket Chart Display Pippa Pig in a pocket chart. Say her name, emphasizing the /p/ sound slightly, and have children echo this.

3 📼 **Alphafriend Audiotape** Play Pippa Pig's song. Listen for /p/ words.

4 Alphafolder Children name the /p/ pictures in the illustration.

5 Summarize

■ *What is our Alphafriend's name? What is her sound?*

■ *What words in our Alphafriend's song start with /p/?*

■ *Each time you look at Pippa Pig this week, remember the /p/ sound.*

Pippa Pig's Song
(tune: Hush! Little Baby)

Pippa had a party
  for Porcupine.
Panda and Penguin
  came to dine.
Pippa served pizza
  and pasta, too.
Pieces of peaches
  and a pickle stew.

▶ Listening for / p /

Compare and Review: / n /, / c / Display Alphafriends *Nyle Noodle* and *Callie Cat* opposite *Pippa Pig.* Review each character's sound.

Hold up Picture Cards one at a time. Children signal "thumbs up" for pictures that start with Pippa Pig's sound, / p /. Volunteers put the card below Pippa's picture. For "thumbs down" words, volunteers put cards below the correct Alphafriends.

Pictures: *can, cot, cow, net, nine, nurse, peach, pot, purse*

Tell children that they will sort more pictures in the Phonics Center today.

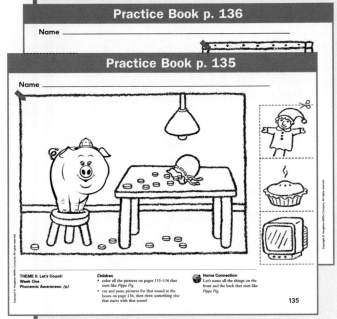

▶ Apply

Practice Book pages 135–136 Children will complete the pages at small group time.

At Group Time

Phonics Center

Use the Phonics Center materials for **Theme 5, Week 1, Day 1**.

High-Frequency Word Practice

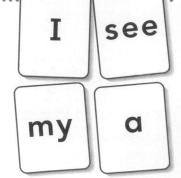

▶ Matching Words

■ Display Word Cards for the high-frequency words *I, see, my, a* in a pocket chart. Call on children to identify each word and to match it on the Word Wall.

■ Remind children that these words are often found in books. *I'll read a poem. You listen to hear if these words are used in it.*

■ Read the poem "One, Two, Three, Four, Five" on page 22 of *Higglety Pigglety.* ***Did you hear any of these words in the poem? Let's see which Word Cards you can match to the words in the poem.***

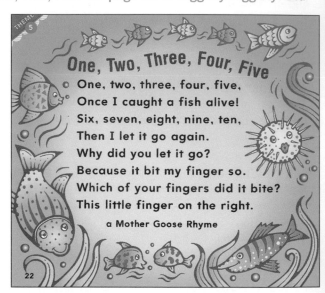

Higglety Pigglety: A Book of Rhymes, **page 22**

Writing Opportunity Have children use Word and Picture Cards to make sentences. Children may then write and illustrate one of the sentences or use the words to create their own sentences with rebus pictures. Children can use temporary phonics spellings in their writing.

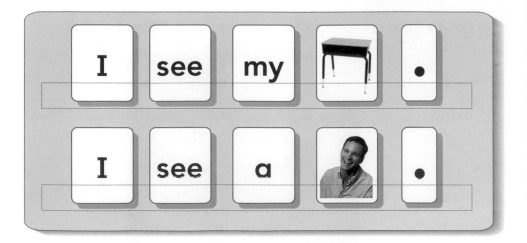

Oral Language

▶ **Using Describing Words**

Listening, Viewing, and Speaking Review that describing words tell how something looks or tell how many.

- Tell children that they will now play a guessing game called "I See." To play, explain that you will use numbers and colors to describe something in the room. Children will then try to guess what you see, for example: *I see one brown* _____.

I see 1 brown
I see 2 red
I see 3 yellow

- Write children's responses on chart paper.

- Provide a few sentence examples before calling on volunteers to continue the game by describing items by number and color for classmates to name.

Portfolio Opportunity

Save children's number and color descriptions for their portfolios to indicate their understanding of one-to-one correspondence.

At Group Time

Writing Center

Materials • drawing paper • markers

Put the chart from above in the Writing Center. Children can refer to the chart as needed. Have them draw individual pictures to illustrate a sentence of their choosing. Some children will be able to label their drawings with color and number words.

4 yellow

Day at a Glance

Learning to Read

Big Book:

Feast for 10

☑ **Phonics:**
Initial
Consonant *p,*
page T20

☑ **High-**
Frequency
Word: *and,*
page T22

Word Work

High-Frequency Word Practice,
page T24

Writing & Language

Vocabulary Expansion, *page T25*

Half-Day Kindergarten

☑ Indicates lessons for tested skills. Choose additional activities as time allows.

Opening

Calendar

Sunday	Monday	Tuesday	Wednesday	Thursday	Friday	Saturday
			1	2	3	4
5	6	7	8	9	10	11
12	13	14	15	16	17	18
19	20	21	22	23	24	25
26	27	28	29	30	31	

If you haven't already done so, begin tracking the day's weather on the calendar. Then ask questions to help children practice number words and quantities: *How many sunny days have we had this month? How many rainy days? Have we have* **more** *or* **fewer** *sunny days than rainy days?*

Daily Message

Modeled Writing Have children provide the initial consonants for words beginning with known sounds: *The first word I want to write is* Today. *What sound do you hear at the beginning of* today? (/t/) *What letter do I write to spell this sound?* (t) Write *Today*, pointing out that the first word in a sentence always begins with a capital letter.

Today we will
make popcorn.

Distribute Word Cards for the words on the Word Wall. Have children match the cards to the words on the Word Wall. After a match is made, have children chant the spelling of the word: **a-t** *spells* **at.**

Daily Phonemic Awareness

Blending Onset and Rime

- Tell children that you are thinking of a number word and ask them to guess it. Say the word, segmenting it by onset and rime: / *f* // *ive* / (five); / *n* // *ine* / (nine); / *s* // *ix* /(six). Continue with these one syllable number words: *two, four, ten.*

- Give children time to think, then hold up corresponding numeral cards so they can check their responses.

Getting Ready to Learn

To help plan their day, tell children that they will

- listen to a Big Book: *Feast for 10.*

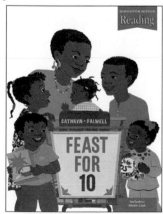

- learn the new letters, *P, p,* and see words that begin with *p.*

- sort foods into food groups in the Science Center.

HOUGHTON MIFFLIN
Reading

CATHRYN FALWELL

FEAST FOR 10

Includes:
Math Link

Purposes • concepts of print • story language
• reading strategy • comprehension skill

Selection Summary

This counting story takes a family, from one to ten, through a shopping trip to the grocery store and from one to ten again as they prepare and eat a feast.

Key Concepts

Number words
Food groups

Sharing the Big Book
Oral Language/Comprehension

▶ Building Background

Introduce the Big Book by reading the title and the names of the author and illustrator. Discuss what children know about feasts, or special meals. Begin a graphic organizer to help children list their favorite "feast" foods.
Save the chart for children to add to after the story.

Meat and Fish
turkey, pork chops

Dairy
milk, cheese

Favorite Feast Foods

Sweets
pie

Fruit and Vegetables
potatoes, peas

Bread and Grains
noodles, rice

Strategy: Monitor/Clarify

Teacher Modeling Preview the pictures on the first few pages of the book. Pause on pages 4 and 5 to model the Monitor/Clarify strategy.

Think Aloud

Sometimes when I read, I may read things I don't understand. One thing I can do to check my understanding is to look at the pictures.

When I look at these pictures, I see the number 2 and two pumpkins. I also see the number 3 and three chickens. This helps me understand that this is a counting book.

✓ Comprehension: Categorize and Classify

Teacher Modeling Remind children that good readers think about ways they can group different things in a story.

Think Aloud

As I read, I'll think about the different kinds of food the family buys. I'll think about the kinds of foods they are. You think about that, too.

▶ Sharing the Story

Read the selection aloud, tracking the print with a pointer or your hand and pointing out the numerals and number words. Pause for children to name the numeral on each page before reading the text.

▶ Responding

Personal Response Encourage children to use the language of the story as they react to it.

■ *What did you like best about the story?*

■ *What foods did the family buy that are like the foods that your family buys?*

■ *What things did the family do together? How did the different family members help one another?*

■ *Did you think about food groups as you listened to the story? What foods did the family buy? Help me add these foods to our chart.*

Literature Circle Have children compare how the family in the story shops and prepares for a feast to the way in which their families shop and prepare for a special meal.

At Group Time

Science Center

Materials • five shoe boxes • food magazines and grocery store circulars • scissors

Prepare five shoe boxes, one for each food group, by pasting pictures of foods from each target group on the appropriate box. Then have children look through food magazines and grocery circulars to find and cut out pictures of foods. Tell children to work with partners to decide in which box each picture should be placed.

MEETING INDIVIDUAL NEEDS **Extra Support**

Place a food pyramid chart in the Science Center and refer children to it as you help children name the foods in the story.

OBJECTIVES

Children

- identify words that begin with /p/
- identify pictures whose names begin with *p*
- form the letters *P, p*

MATERIALS

- **Alphafriend Card** *Pippa Pig*
- **Letter Cards** *p, n, c*
- **Picture Cards** for *p, n,* and *c*
- **Blackline Master 172**
- **Phonics Center:** Theme 5, Week 1, Day 2

Extra Support

To help children remember the sound for *p*, point out that the letter's name gives a clue to its sound: *p*, /p/.

Phonics

✔ Initial Consonant p

▶ Develop Phonemic Awareness

Beginning Sound Read this poem aloud, and have children echo it line-for-line. Have them listen for the /p/ words and "pop up" for each one.

Pippa Pig's Song
(tune: Hush! Little Baby)
Pippa had a party
    for Porcupine.
Panda and Penguin
    came to dine.
Pippa served pizza
    and pasta, too.
Pieces of peaches
    and a pickle stew.

▶ Connect Sounds to Letters

Beginning Letter Display the *Pippa Pig* card, and have children name the letter on the picture. Say, *The letter **p** stands for the sound /p/, as in **pig**. When you see a **p**, remember **Pippa Pig**. That will help you remember the sound /p/.*

Write *pig* on the board. Underline the *p*. *What is the first letter in the word* **pig?**
(p) **Pig** *starts with /p/, so* **p** *is the first letter I write for* **pig.**

Compare and Review: *n, c*
In a pocket chart, display the Letter Cards as shown and the Picture Cards in random order. Review the sounds for *p, n,* and *c.* In turn, children can name a picture, say the beginning sound, and put the cards below the right letter. Tell children they will sort more pictures in the Phonics Center today.

▶ Handwriting

Writing *P, p* Tell children that now they'll learn to write the letters that stand for / p /: capital *P* and small *p*. Write each letter as you recite the handwriting rhyme. Children can chant each rhyme as they "write" the letter in the air.

Handwriting Rhyme: P

Start at the top and make a long line down.
Go back to the top and circle half-way around.

Handwriting Rhyme: p

Start in the middle and make a long line down.
Go back to the middle and circle half-way around.

▶ Apply

Practice Book page 137 Children will complete the page at small group time.

Blackline Master 172 This page provides additional handwriting practice.

At Group Time

Phonics Center

Use the Phonics Center materials for **Theme 5, Week 1, Day 2**.

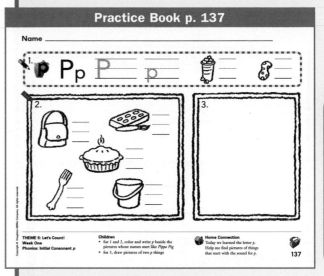

Practice Book p. 137

Teacher's Note

Handwriting practice for the continuous stroke style is available on **Blackline Master 198**.

Portfolio Opportunity
Add children's handwriting samples to their portfolios.

OBJECTIVES

CHILDREN

- read and write the high-frequency word *and*

MATERIALS

- **Word Cards** *a, and, I, like, see, to*
- **Picture Cards** *hop, pan, pot, run, toast, watermelon*
- **Punctuation Card:** period
- **Higglety Pigglety: A Book of Rhymes,** page 10

✅ High-Frequency Word

New Word: and

▶ **Teach**

Tell children that today they will learn to read and write a word that they will often see in stories. Say *and* and use it in context.

I drink milk *and* juice.   I like cats *and* dogs.   I like to sing *and* dance.

Write *and* on the board, and have children spell it as you point to the letter. **Spell and with me, a-n-d.** Then lead children in a chant, clapping on each beat, to help them remember that *and* is spelled a-n-d: **a-n-d, *and*! a-n-d, *and*.**

Word Wall   Ask children to help you decide where on the Word Wall *and* should be posted. As needed, prompt children by pointing out that *and* begins with the letter *a*. Have children find and read the *a* words already on the Word Wall *(a, an, at)* and then add *and*. Remind children to look there when they need to remember how to write the word.

▶ **Practice**

Reading Build the following sentences in a pocket chart. Have children take turns reading the sentences aloud. Children can practice building and reading sentences in the pocket chart in small group time.

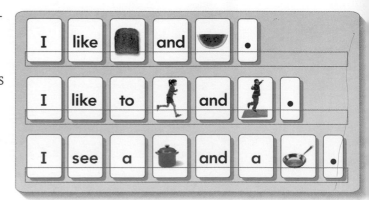

Display *Higglety Pigglety: A Book of Rhymes*, page 10.

■ Share the poem "I Love Colors" aloud.

■ Reread the second line of the poem. *I'll read the second line again. This time I'll read it slowly. You listen for the word* and. *If you hear it raise your hand.* Repeat with the last line of the poem.

■ Call on children to point to the word *and* each time it appears in the poem.

Higglety Pigglety: A Book of Rhymes, page 10

Practice Book p. 138

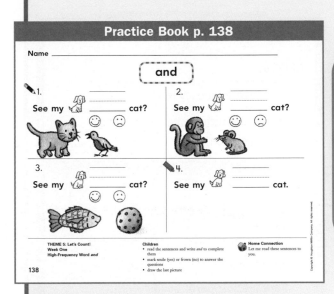

··

▶ **Apply**

Practice Book page 138 Children will read and write *and* as they complete the Practice Book page. On Day 3 they will practice reading *and* in the **Phonics Library** story "Nat, Pat, and Nan."

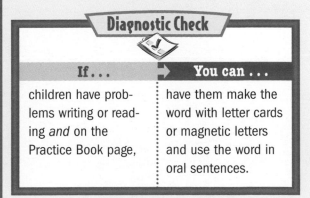
High-Frequency Words

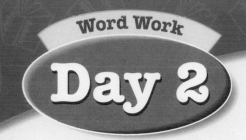

Day 2

Word Work

OBJECTIVES

Children

- read high-frequency words
- create and write sentences with high-frequency words

MATERIALS

- **Word Cards** *a, and, I, like*
- **Picture Cards** *jam, peach, sandwich, toast, watermelon*
- **Punctuation Card:** *period*
- **Additional pictures of foods:** *chicken, eggs, fish, ham, milk, juice* (optional)

High-Frequency Word Practice

▶ **Building Sentences**

Tell children that you want to build a sentence about foods people like.

- Display the Word and Picture Cards in random order. Put the Word Card *I* in the pocket chart, and read it.

- *I want the next word to be* like. *Who can find that word? That's right! This word is* like. *Now who can read my sentence so far?*

- Continue building the sentence *I like* _____ *and* _____. Children choose Picture Cards for the blanks.

- Read the completed sentence together.

✏ **Writing Opportunity** Have children write the sentence from above or they can choose their own food words and add drawings. Remind them to use temporary phonics spellings by saying words slowly and writing the letters they hear.

Vocabulary Expansion

▶ **Using Number Words**

- Remind children that number words tell how many. Briefly review number words by asking questions such as: *How many hands do you have? How many noses do you have? How many fingers are on one hand? How many children are wearing blue shirts?*

- Display the number chart on page 28 and review it with children.

- Make a number page using pictures of foods. On chart paper, write the numerals and number words for 1–10. Then brainstorm foods to include on the chart. Children can help illustrate the chart with the appropriate number of food items.

Numbers

1	one	
2	two	
3	three	
4	four	
5	five	
6	six	
7	seven	
8	eight	
9	nine	
10	ten	

28

Apples to Zebras: A Book of ABC's, page 28

1	one	pumpkin
2	two	apples
3	three	carrots
4	four	bananas

At Group Time
Art Center

Write the numerals 1 to 5 on several sheets of paper and put them in the Art Center. At small group time, children can complete the activity by writing number words and adding drawings of foods or other items.

1 one

OBJECTIVES

Children
- use number words

MATERIALS

- *Apples to Zebras: A Book of ABC's,* page 28

DAY 2

MEETING INDIVIDUAL NEEDS **Challenge**

Many foods begin with the target sound and letter,/ p /, p. Challenge children to complete their number charts using only those foods whose names begin with / p /: *pizza, peanuts, peas, peppers, potatoes, pumpkin, pineapple, pretzels, pasta, pancakes, peach, pear, pie, popcorn, papaya.*

Day at a Glance

Learning to Read

Big Book:

Feast for 10

✓ **Phonics:**
Blending *p*
-*an*, page
T34

Word Work

✓ **Building Words**, *page T36*

Writing & Language

Shared Writing, *page T37*

Half-Day Kindergarten

✓ Indicates lessons for tested skills. Choose additional activities as time allows.

Calendar

Sunday	Monday	Tuesday	Wednesday	Thursday	Friday	Saturday
			1	2	3	4
5	6	7	8	9	10	11
12	13	14	15	16	17	18
19	20	21	22	23	24	25
26	27	28	29	30	31	

Continue to use the calendar to practice identifying numbers and counting. Mark the day of a class party, trip, or other special event and have children count the days until the event takes place.

Daily Message

Modeled Writing Explain what you are doing as you write the daily message: *The next word I am going to write is* **night**. *Listen as I say the word again,* **night**. *What letter should I write to write the first letter in* **night**? (n) *The last letter in* **night** *is* **t**. *I'll leave a space before I write the first letter in the next word.*

Last night I ate tacos for dinner. What did you eat?

Word Wall

Choose a volunteer to point to and read two words that are made up of only one letter. (a, I) Then ask volunteers to find and read the words that are made up of two letters. (an, at, my, to) Have children name the first and last letter in each of these words. Continue until all the words have been read.

Routines

✓ Daily Phonemic Awareness

Blending Onset and Rime

- Play "Pat, Pat, Clap" with these words.

- Children follow the routine. They pat for the onset and the rime. Then they clap for the words. / h / (pat); / am / (pat); and *ham* (clap). Demonstrate a few times and get children into the rhythm of the game.

Pat, Pat, Clap

soup	bean	milk
ham	rice	peas
lime	cake	nut
toast	jam	bun
corn	fish	

Getting Ready to Learn

To help plan their day, tell children that they will

- reread and talk about the Big Book: *Feast for 10.*

- read a story called "Nat, Pat, and Nan."

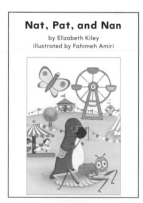

- read, write, and explore favorite foods in the Art Center.

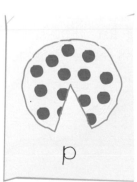

Day 3

Sharing the Big Book

OBJECTIVES

Children

- listen to a Big Book
- distinguish between letter and word
- identify the first and last letter in words

Big Book

CATHRYN FALWELL

FEAST FOR 10

Reading for Understanding Reread the story, emphasizing number words and rhyme. Pause for Supporting Comprehension points.

 Extra Support

Provide additional practice with numbers and counting by having children count the items mentioned on each page. This will also help children verify the connection between the pictures and the text.

1 one cart into the grocery store

pages 2-3

2 two pumpkins for pie

3 three chickens to fry

pages 4–5

4 four children off to look for more

pages 6–7

pages 8–9

pages 10–11

pages 12–13

▶ **Supporting Comprehension**

pages 2–3

Strategy: Monitor/Clarify

Teacher-Student Modeling Review how pictures and words can help clarify understanding of a book. Prompts:

- *What do you see that helps you understand that this is a counting book? Do you remember how many times this story counts to ten?*

page 4

Drawing Conclusions

- *What kind of pie do you think the family will make? How do you know?*

pages 6–7

Noting Details

- *How do the children help at the grocery store?*
  (looking for items, gathering items for the cart)

Revisiting the Text

pages 8–9

✓ Comprehension Focus: Categorize and Classify

Teacher-Student Modeling *What kind of beans do you see?* (lima, pinto, string, green, and jelly) *Beans are vegetables. Which of these beans are not vegetables?* (jelly beans)

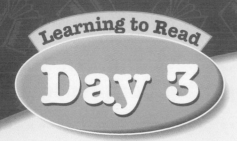

pages 14–15

▶ ## Supporting Comprehension

pages 14–15

Strategy: Monitor/Clarify

Teacher-Student Modeling Recall that good readers check their understanding of a story as they read. Prompts:

- *What could you do if you didn't understand what "ten hands help to load the car" means?* (look at the pictures)

pages 14–15

Noting Details

- *What symbol is on the grocery bags? What does it mean to recycle?* (to save a thing to be used again or made into something else)

Revisiting the Text

pages 18–19

Concepts of Print

 Letter/Word

- *How many words are on page 18?* (three) Call on a volunteer to frame the first word. *How many letters are in this word? Most words are made up of more than one letter. Can you think of a word that has only one letter in it? Look at the Word Wall if you need help.* (I, a)

pages 16–17

pages 18–19

four
will
taste
and ask
for
more

20

pages 20–21

five
empty
cans

six
pots and
pans

22   23

pages 22–23

seven
more carrots
to wash
and
peel

24   25

pages 24–25

▶ **Supporting Comprehension**

pages 20–21

Drawing Conclusions

■ *What are the children tasting? Do you think they like the pie filling? What makes you think so?*

pages 22–23

Making Judgments

■ *Does this family recycle? How do you know? Do you think everyone should recycle? Why?*

pages 24–25

Comprehension Focus: Categorize and Classify

Student Modeling Have children name the food on pages 24 and 25 and tell to which food group carrots belong. Revisit the pictures in the story to name and categorize other foods for their feast and categorize these items. Discuss children's decisions.

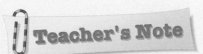 **Teacher's Note**

Language Patterns

Rhyme This book has a strong rhyme scheme. On a rereading, point out the rhyming pairs or pause for children to supply the rhyming words.

 Challenge

MEETING INDIVIDUAL NEEDS

Some children will be able to find specific words that you choose and read them to a partner.

DAY 3

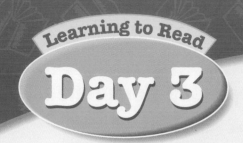

pages 26–27

▶ **Supporting Comprehension**

pages 28–29

Strategy: Monitor/Clarify

Student Modeling Recall that on the previous page nine chairs were placed at the table.

■ *Here, it says ten folks share the meal. What can you do if you are confused about the number of chairs and the number of people? How do the pictures help you?* (The baby, the tenth person, is sitting in someone's lap, not a chair.)

pages 28–29

Vocabulary

platters: A platter is a large serving dish.

folks: Another word for people, usually people who belong to the same group, like a family.

Revisiting the Text

pages 28–29

Concepts of Print

 First/Last Letter Word

■ How many words are on page 29? (seven) Frame the first word. *This is the word* ten. *What is the first letter in* ten? *What is the last letter in the word?* Repeat the procedure with the word *meal*. Explain to children that the letters in a word are read in the same direction as the words in a sentence, from left to right.

page 30

▶ Responding

Retelling Use prompts to help children summarize the selection:

■ ***What happened the first time we counted from one to ten?*** (The family shopped for the feast.)

■ ***What happened in the second half of the book; the second time we counted from one to ten?*** (The family prepared for the feast.)

■ ***What were some of the different kinds of foods the family bought and prepared?***

Practice Book page 139 Children will complete the page at small group time.

Literature Circle Have small groups discuss what might happen if the book were to continue and begin counting from one to ten again. ***What might the family do this time?*** (Children might suggest clean up from the feast.)

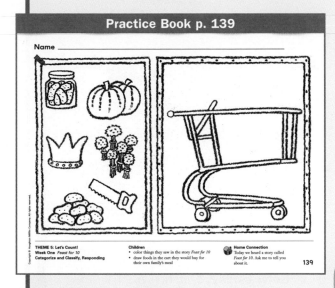

At Group Time

Art Center

Materials • drawing paper • food group pictures from Science Center • glue

Prepare place settings on drawing paper as shown. Write *My Perfect Meal* across the top. Have children plan a feast by choosing choices from each food group. Children then arrange and paste the food pictures onto the "plates." Encourage children to label their favorite foods.

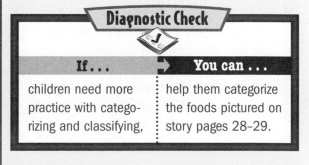

MEETING INDIVIDUAL NEEDS

English Language Learners

Children may not have heard the word *folks*. Point to the word, read it aloud, and have children say the word after you. Check to make sure they are not saying the word with an *l*. Ask if anyone knows a word that could fit here instead of *folks*. (people) Reread the page, substituting the word *people*.

Diagnostic Check

If...	You can...
children need more practice with categorizing and classifying,	help them categorize the foods pictured on story pages 28–29.

DAY 3

Practice Book p. 140

Extra Support

Read "Peter Piper," **Higglety Pigglety: A Book of Rhymes,** page 23. Have children pat their legs each time they hear a word that begins with /p/. Then ask volunteers to point to words that begin with /p/. Read the words aloud and have children repeat them as they listen for the beginning sound.

Phonics

✓ *Blending p -an*

▶ **Connect Sounds to Letters**

Review Consonant *p* Play Pippa Pig's song, and have children clap for each /p/ word. Write *P* and *p* on the board, and list words from the song.

Blending -at Tell children that they'll build a word with *p*, but first they'll need a vowel ("helper letter"). Display Alphafriend *Andy Apple*.

Who remembers this character name? Yes, this is Andy Apple. *Say* Andy Apple *with me. Andy's letter is the vowel* a, *and the sound* a *usually stands for is /ă/.* Hold up the Letter Card *a.* *You say /ă/. Listen for the /ă/ sound in these words: /ă/ and, /ă/ ask, /ă/ at.*

Hold up the Letter Cards *a* and *n*. Remind children that they know the sound for *n*. Model blending the sounds as you hold the cards apart and then together: */ă / /n/, an. I've made the word* an. *The sound for* a *is first, and the sound for* n *is last.* Have volunteers move the cards as classmates blend.

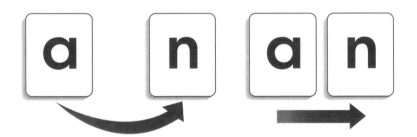

 Add *an* to the Word Wall. Children will use *an* to make other words.

Blending -an Words Build *an* in a pocket chart. Then put *p* in front of *an*, and model blending /p/ /an/, *pan*. Have children blend the sounds while you point.

▶ **Apply**

Practice Book page 140 Children complete the page at small group time.

Phonics in Action

Reading
Phonics Library

Let's Count!

Applying Phonics Skills and High-Frequency Words

Purposes
- apply phonics skills
- apply high-frequency words

Nat, Pat, and Nan
by Elizabeth Kiley
illustrated by Fahimeh Amiri

1

> ## Phonics/Decoding Strategy
>
> **Teacher Modeling** Discuss using the Phonics/Decoding strategy to read words in the story.
>
> ### Think Aloud
>
> *The last word in the title begins with capital N. The sound for N is / n /. I know the sounds for a, n: / ă // n /, an /. Let's blend: / n // an /, Nan. Is Nan the name of a person? Does it make sense here?*

Do a picture walk. Show children that Pat ran on page 3. Write *ran* on the board and model blending / r // an /, *ran*. Ask one child to point and model the blending.

Nat sat.

2

Pat ran.
Pat sat.

3

▶ Coached Reading

Have children read each page silently before reading with you. Prompts:

page 2 *What is Nat doing?*

page 4 Choose a child to model how he or she blended *Nan*.

page 5 *What word on this page rhymes with ran?* (Nan) *What letters are the same in those rhyming words?* (a, n as in an) *Could this story really happen?*

Pat and Nat see Nan.
Nan! Nan!

4

Pat, Nat, and Nan sat.

5

Home Connection

Children can color the pictures in their take-home version of the story "Nat, Pat, and Nan." After rereading the story on Day 4, they can take it home and read it to family members.

Phonics (T35)

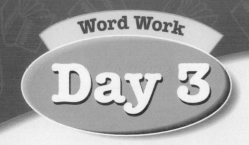

OBJECTIVES

- blend initial consonants with -an to read words

MATERIALS

- **Letter Cards** a, c, m, N, n, p, r, t, v

Building Words

▶ Word Family: -an

Using the Letter Cards, model how to build *an*. *First I'll stretch out the sounds: /ă/.../n/. How many sounds do you hear? The first sound is /ă/. I'll put up an a to spell that. The last sound is /n/. What letter should I choose for that?*

Blend /ă/ and /n/ and read *an*. Then ask which letter you should add to build *pan*. Model how to read *pan* by blending /p/ with /an/.

Then replace *p* with *m* and say: *Now what happens if I change /p/ to /m/?* Continue making and blending *-an* words by substituting *c, N, r, t,* and *v.* List these words on a chart and post it in the Writing Center. Add new words to the *-an* chart as initial consonants are learned.

Have small groups work together to build *-an* words. They can use alphabet beads, block letters, letter magnets, or other manipulatives in your collection.

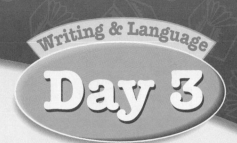

Shared Writing

▶ Writing a List

Recall how the family shopped for groceries for the feast for ten. Tell children that they will write a class grocery list to prepare for a make-believe feast.

- Help children recall some of the items from *Feast for 10* by paging through the book.

- Have children brainstorm items for a make-believe class feast. Record their ideas on a chart as a shared writing experience, having children verbalize initial consonants where appropriate. Suggest that children use numbers in their list.

Class Grocery List
2 pumpkins
5 beans
1 can of soup
6 greens
7 pickles
1 pan

Day 4

Day at a Glance

Learning to Read

Big Book:

What's on the Menu?

✔ **Phonics:** Reviewing / p /; Blending *-an* words, *page T42*

Word Work

✔ **Building Words,** *page T44*

Writing & Language

Interactive Writing, *page T45*

Half-Day Kindergarten

✔ Indicates lessons for tested skills. Choose additional activities as time allows.

Opening

Calendar

Sunday	Monday	Tuesday	Wednesday	Thursday	Friday	Saturday
			1	2	3	4
5	6	7	8	9	10	11
12	13	14	15	16	17	18
19	20	21	22	23	24	25
26	27	28	29	30	31	

Practice number words and counting by conducting countdowns to different events throughout the month. Choose a target date, put your finger on that date, and count to reach the current date. Then count down, or backwards, to reach the target date again.

Daily Message

Interactive Writing As you write the message, call on volunteers to supply the first and last letters in words. Have children share any news they may have by dictating and sharing in the writing with you. In the example shown, Paul might write his own name and supply the initial consonants for *has, new,* and *sister.*

Paul has a new baby sister.

Read the Word Wall together, then play a rhyming game: *I'm going to find a word on the wall that rhymes with cat. Cat rhymes with... at. Raise your hand when you find a word that rhymes with man.* (an)

Routines

✔ Daily Phonemic Awareness

Blending Onset and Rime

- Read "Hickory Dickory Dock" on page 24.

- Play a guessing game. *Let's put some sounds together to make words from the poem: /d//ock/dock. Now you put the sounds for /r/ and /an/ together. What do you get?* (ran)

- Continue the game, by having children blend the sounds /m/, /p/, /t/, /v/, and /k/ with /an/. After each onset-rime, allow children to blend the sounds independently. Then call on a volunteer to blend the sounds aloud.

Hickory Dickory Dock

Hickory dickory dock,
The mouse ran up the clock.
The clock struck one,
The mouse ran down.
Hickory dickory dock.

a Traditional Chant

Higglety Pigglety: A Book of Rhymes, page 24

Getting Ready to Learn

To help plan their day, tell children that they will

- read the Math Link: *What's on the Menu?*

- learn to make and read new words.

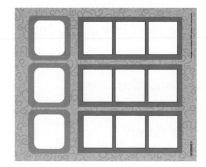

- reread a story called "Nat, Pat, and Nan."

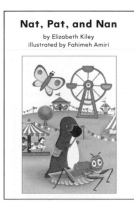

Nat, Pat, and Nan
by Elizabeth Kiley
illustrated by Fahimeh Amiri

DAY 4

Big Book

pages 31-37

Oral Language

menu A menu is a list of foods and drinks. What might be on a breakfast menu?

English Language Learners

Show children samples of menus, especially those that include photographs of food. Ask: "What's this?" Write and say the word *menu*. Have children repeat the word. Ask: "What do you eat for breakfast?" Encourage children to use the picture dictionary and say the words.

Sharing the Big Book
Math Link

▶ Building Background

Display the title page and read the title aloud. Have children name places where they have ordered food from menus. Ask how eating at a restaurant and getting food from another kind of food vendor is different than eating at home.

Reading for Understanding Pause for discussion as you share the selection.

---

page 32

Strategy: Monitor/Clarify

Student Modeling Say that each page tells something important to the article. Read the first line, pointing as you read. Ask: *What can you do if you don't know what the word* diner *means?* (look at the picture)

✓ Comprehension Focus: Categorize and Classify

Student Modeling The second sentence says to pick four breakfast treats. Ask: *How does knowing how to group things that are alike help you choose four breakfast treats? Which food item is not usually eaten for breakfast?* (hamburger)

---

page 33

Drawing Conclusions

- *What is a cafe? How do you know?*

page 34

Compare and Contrast

- *What do you have for a snack? How is a snack different from a breakfast, lunch, or dinner?*

Breakfast

We can have breakfast
at the diner!
Pick four breakfast treats.

32

LUNCH

We can have lunch
at the cafe!
Pick five lunchtime treats.

33

pages 32–33

Snack

We can have a snack
at the snack cart!
Pick three snack treats.

34

DINNER

We can have dinner
at the restaurant!
Pick five dinner treats.

35

pages 34–35

What foods and drinks
do you like most?

36

Make a menu!

37

pages 36–37

pages 34—35

Concepts of Print

 Letter/Word; First/Last Letter in a Word

■ With your hand, frame the sentence *Pick three snack treats.* Ask: *How many words do you see?*

■ Frame the first word. *This word is* pick. *What is the first letter in the word* pick? *The last letter? Show me the same word on page 35.*

▶ Responding

Summarizing Ask children to answer the question on page 36. Then have them retell the selection in their own words, using the photographs as prompts.

 Extra Support

Some children may not be familiar with the food vendors shown. If so, guide children to discuss diners, cafes, food carts, and restaurants.

 Challenge

Prepare cards for the words and end marks for one or two sentences from the selection. One child builds a sentence and reads it with a partner.

DAY 4

Sharing the Big Book T41

Teacher's Note

When writing children may ask how to spell words from the *-an* family. Help children find the word *an* on the Word Wall and add the appropriate initial consonant(s).

Home Connection

Challenge children to look at home for items or for names that begin with the consonant *p*. Children can draw pictures to show what they have found.

Phonics

✅ *Blending -an Words*

▶ Connect Sounds to Letters

Review Consonant *p* Using self stick notes, cover the words on page 17 of **Apples to Zebras: A Book of ABC's.** Then display the page. Ask children to name each picture and tell what letter they expect to see first in each word and why. Uncover the words so that children can check their predictions.

Apples to Zebras: A Book of ABC's, page 17

Reviewing *-an* Remind children that to build some words with *p*, they also need a vowel ("helper letter"), because every word has at least one of those. Ask which Alphafriend stands for the vowel sound /ă/. (Andy Apple) Display Andy and have children think of other words that start with /ă/. (*ant, act, alligator, and, at*)

Hold up Letter Cards *a* and *n*. ***Watch and listen as I build a word from the Word Wall:*** /ă//n/, *an,* /ă//n/, *an.*

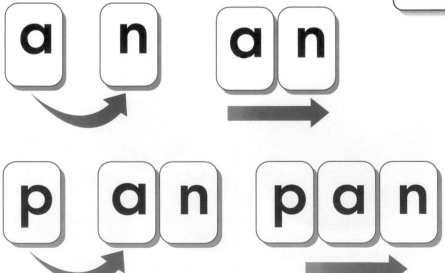

Blending *-an* Words Put Letter Card *p* in front of *an.* ***Now let's blend my new word:*** /p//an/, **pan.** Continue, having volunteers build and blend *man, Nan, ran,* and *tan.*

▶ Apply

In a pocket chart, display the Picture Card for *pan*. Have children say *pan* with you, stretching out the sounds. Build the word *pan* in the pocket chart.

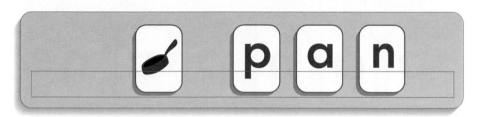

Then build *van* and *can*. Choose children to read the *-an* words. Monitor responses. Tell children they will build more words in the Phonics Center today.

Practice Book page 141 Children will complete this page at small group time.

Phonics Library In groups today, children will also read *-an* words as they reread the **Phonics Library** story "Nat, Pat, and Nan." See suggestions, page T35.

Use the Phonics Center materials for **Theme 5, Week 1, Day 4**.

Practice Book p. 141

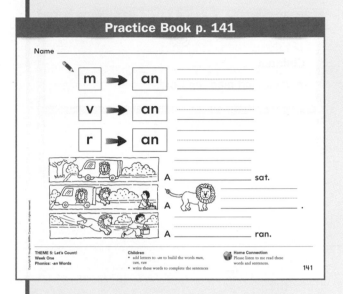

DAY 4

Extra Support

Children who have difficulty blending can be helped by slowing down a word. Have them pretend to "stretch taffy" for each word. S-T-R-E-T-C-H a word to show them how.

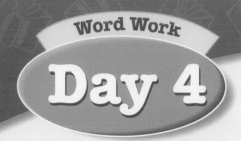

MATERIALS

- **Letter Cards** *a, b, c, h, m, N, n, p, r, s, t, v*

Building Words

▶ Word Families: *-at, -an*

Model how to build *an* in a pocket chart, saying the sounds slowly. ***Let's build the word*** **pan. *Which letter should I put in front of*** **an?**

Tell children that you will now replace the *p* with other letters they've learned (*c, m, N, r, t, v*) to build more *-an* words.

Ask if children remember another word family they've learned. Use letter cards to build *at.* ***First I'll stretch out the sounds. /ă/.../t/. How many sounds do you hear? The first sound is /ă/. I'll put up an a to spell that. The last sound is /t/. What letter should I choose for that?***

Blend /ă/ and /t/ to read *at.* Ask which letter you should add to build *pat.* Model how to read *pat* by blending /p/ with /at/. Then replace *p* with *b* and say: ***Now what happens if I change /p/ to /b/?*** Continue making and blending *-at* words by substituting *c, h, m, r, s.* Be sure to monitor children who are struggling to learn the sounds of the letters.

– an	– at
can	cat
Nan	hat
ran	mat
tan	rat
van	sat

Challenge

Children who can blend words with *-an* easily can create a personal word bank of *-an* words in their journals.

Interactive Writing

▶ Writing a List

Viewing and Speaking Show children pages 32–35 of *What's on the Menu?* and have children name some of the foods they see. Discuss how they have learned two ways to sort foods—by group and by meal.

- Display the graphic organizer from yesterday's shared writing. Review the list, and invite children to suggest additional items.

- Continue adding items to the list. Or start a new list, charting food items that children like. Point out how to write from the top to the bottom of the page.

- Follow the routine for interactive writing. If a suggested word begins or ends with a known consonant, choose a child to write the letter. For any words that rhyme with *at* or *an*, ask another child to write those letters.

At Group Time

Writing Center

Put the Class Grocery List in the Writing Center. Children can refer to the chart when drawing pictures of a favorite meal. Then children can create grocery lists for their meal by copying items from the list or by adding their own items.

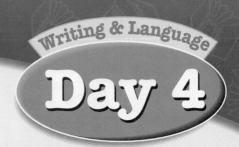

OBJECTIVES

Children
- participate in interactive writing

MATERIALS
- **Big Book:** *What's on the Menu?* pages 32-35

Portfolio Opportunity

Children may wish to add their grocery lists to their portfolios as an indication of their knowledge of numerals and number words.

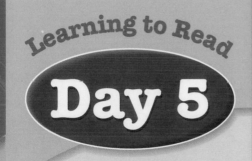
Day at a Glance

Learning to Read

Revisiting the Literature:

Benny's Pennies, Feast for 10, What's on the Menu?, "Nat, Pat, and Nan"

☑ **Phonics: Initial Consonants p, n, c; Blending -at, -an words;** *page T50*

Word Work

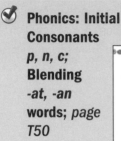

☑ **Building Words,** *page T52*

Writing & Language

Independent Writing, *page T53*

 Half-Day Kindergarten

☑ Indicates lessons for tested skills. Choose additional activities as time allows.

Opening

Calendar

Sunday	Monday	Tuesday	Wednesday	Thursday	Friday	Saturday
			1	2	3	4
5	6	7	8	9	10	11
12	13	14	15	16	17	18
19	20	21	22	23	24	25
26	27	28	29	30	31	

Review number words and other words you may have added to the calendar and have children use them in oral sentences.

Daily Message

Interactive Writing Share the pen: In the daily message, occasionally ask a volunteer to contribute words or letter they can read and write.

> Today is Friday. We will go to the aquarium.

Remind children that the words on the Word Wall are in ABC order. *I will say the alphabet, and you raise your hand when I come to a letter that begins a word on the wall. A... Are there any words that begin with a? Who will point to them and read them?*

Routines

Daily Phonemic Awareness

Blending Onset and Rime

- Display Picture Cards for *bat, can, cat, fan, hat, man, mat,* and *van.*

- Say: *I'll say some sounds. You put them together to make words that name the pictures. Listen: / m /... / at /. Who can show me the picture whose name has the sounds / m /... / at /? That's right,* mat. *Say the sounds with me / m /... / at /,* mat.

- Continue the game with the names for the other Picture Cards.

Getting Ready to Learn

To help plan their day, tell children that they will

- reread and talk about all the books they've read this week.

- take home a story they can read.

- write about their favorite foods in their journals.

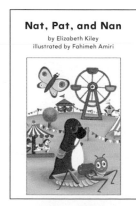

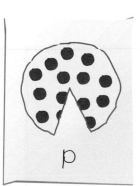

Revisiting the Literature

▶ Literature Discussion

Today children will compare the books you shared this week: *Benny's Pennies, Feast for 10, What's on the Menu?* and "Nat, Pat, and Nan." First, use these suggestions to help children recall the selections:

- Have volunteers tell what gifts Benny bought with his pennies in *Benny's Pennies.*

- Display *Feast for 10.* Recall what the family did the first time the story counted from one to ten (shopped for food) and the second time the story counted from one to ten (prepared for the feast).

- Name one or two places from *What's on the Menu?* (diner, cafe, cart, restaurant). Choose a child to find those places in the book and to describe the kinds of foods that they might find there.

- Together, read "Nat, Pat, and Nan." Ask specific children to explain how they blended *ran*.

- Ask children to vote for their favorite book of the week. Then read the winning book aloud.

✓ Comprehension: Categorize and Classify

Comparing Books   Remind children that grouping information helps readers understand a book. Browse through each selection and talk about the gifts in *Benny's Pennies,* the groups of foods in *Feast for 10,* and the menu of choices in *What's on the Menu?*

www.eduplace.com

Log on to **Education Place** for more activities relating to Let's Count!

www.bookadventure.org

This free Internet reading incentive program provides thousands of titles for students to read.

Building Fluency

▶ Rereading Familiar Texts

Phonics Library: "Nat, Pat, and Nan" Remind children that they've learned the new word *and*, and that they've learned to read words with *-an*. As children reread the **Phonics Library** stories "Nat, Pat, and Nan," and "Cat Sat," and "A Vat," have them look for *-an* and *-at* words.

Review Feature several familiar **Phonics Library** titles in the Book Corner. Have children demonstrate their growing skills by choosing one to reread aloud, alternating pages with a partner. From time to time, choose specific children to point out words or phrases.

Oral Reading Frequent rereadings of familiar texts help children develop the ability to read word groupings more smoothly. Model how to read expressively and in meaningful phrases. Then have children try it.

Nat, Pat, and Nan
by Elizabeth Kiley
illustrated by Fahimeh Amiri

Cat Sat
by Elizabeth Kiley
illustrated by Shari Halpern

A Vat
by Elizabeth Kiley
illustrated by Bob Kolar

Blackline Master 36 Children complete the page and take it home to share their reading progress.

The materials listed below provide reading practice for children at different levels.

Little Big Books

Little Readers for Guided Reading

Houghton Mifflin Classroom Bookshelf

Home Connection

Remind children to share the take-home version of "Nat, Pat, and Nan" with their families.

OBJECTIVES

- build and read words with initial consonants and short *a* + *t*, short *a* + *n*
- make sentences with high-frequency words

MATERIALS

- **Word Cards** *I, see, my, like, a, to, and*
- **Punctuation Cards:** period, question mark

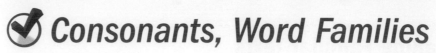

Phonics Review

✔ Consonants, Word Families

▶ Review

Tell children that they will take turns being word builders and word readers today. Have a group of word builders stand with you at the chalkboard. Readers write the words at their places.

Let's build an. *First, count the sounds... I know* a *stands for* /ă/ *and* n *stands for* /n/. Write the letters.

- Children copy *an* from the board and blend the sounds.

- Add *p* in front of your letters. Children write *pan* and ask the rest of the class (word readers) what new word they've made.

- A new group changes places with the first one. At your directions, they erase the *p*, write *m*, and ask the word readers to say the new word.

- Continue by having other children build a word by replacing one letter.

- Examples: *can, Nan, ran, tan, van, bat, Pat, sat, cat, hat, mat, pat, rat.*

- Then have other groups confer and change the first letter on their own. They ask the word readers to write and read the new word.

High-Frequency Word Review
 I, see, my, like, a, to, and

▶ Review

Give each small group the Word Cards, Picture Cards, and Punctuation Card needed to make a sentence. Each child holds one card. Children stand and arrange themselves to make a sentence for others to read.

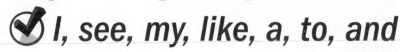

▶ Apply

Practice Book page 142 Children can complete this page independently and read it to you during small group time.

Phonics Library Have children take turns reading aloud to the class. Each child might read one page of "Nat, Pat, and Nan," "Cat Sat," or a favorite **Phonics Library** selection from the previous theme. Remind readers to share the pictures!

Questions for discussion:

- *Do you hear any rhyming words in either story? What letters are the same in those words?*

- *Find a word that starts with the same sound as Pippa Pig's name. What is the letter? What is the sound?*

- *This week we added the word* **and** *to the Word Wall. Find the word* **and** *in "Nat, Pat, and Nan."*

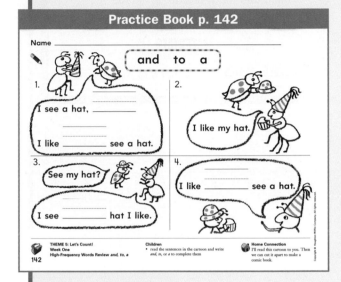

Practice Book p. 142

Portfolio Opportunity

Add the Practice Book page to children's portfolios as a sample of what they have learned.

Diagnostic Check

If...	You can...
children need help remembering the consonant sounds,	have them review the Alphafriends by matching Alphafriend Cards to letter cards.
children pause at high-frequency words in **Phonics Library** selections,	have partners practice reading the words on the Word Wall.

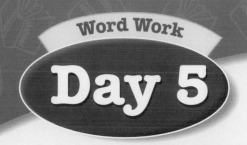

Word Work

Day 5

OBJECTIVES

Children

• build and read *-at* and *-an* words

MATERIALS

• **Letter Cards** *a, b, c, h, m, n, N, p, r, s, t, v*

Building Words

▶ **Word Families:** *-an, -at*

Model how to build *an*. Along the bottom of a pocket chart, line up the letters *m, r, t, c, v,* and *p*. **Let's build the word** man. **Who can tell me which letter I should take from here to make** man? Have a volunteer take the letter *m* and place it in front of *an*. Continue building *-an* words, using initial consonants *r, t, c, v,* and *p*. On chart paper, keep a list of all the *-an* words you make, and reread the list together.

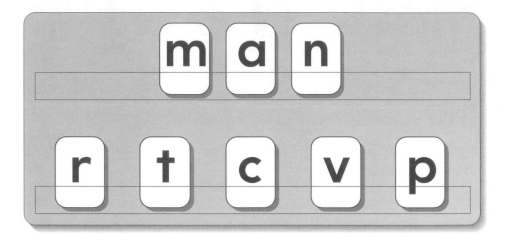

Have small groups work together to build *-at* words with magnetic letters or other alphabet blocks. This time, they can add new words to the Word Bank section of their journals and add appropriate pictures.

Independent Writing

Journals Ask volunteers to read this week's shared and interactive writing posted in the classroom. Point out all ways in which children grouped items and the number words that they used. Tell children that they can use what they've learned to write in their journals about a favorite meal.

- *Let's talk about the things we counted and grouped this week. What kinds of gifts did we group? What kinds of foods did we group? What kinds of foods did we include in our grocery list? What foods would you include on a menu for breakfast? For lunch? How does this help your writing?*

- Remind children that Word Wall words must be spelled correctly. Words in the Writing and Science Centers can help, too. Allow children to also use temporary phonics spellings.

- If time permits, have children share what they've written with the class.

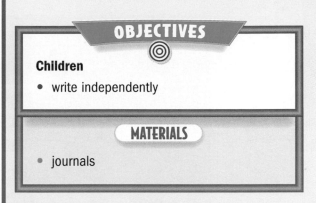

OBJECTIVES

Children
- write independently

MATERIALS
- journals

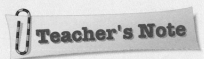

Teacher's Note

Children may enjoy using some of the pictures of foods they cut out from magazines and sorted in the Science Center to illustrate their menus.

Portfolio Opportunity

Mark journal entries you would like to share with parents. Allow children to mark their best efforts or favorite works for sharing as well.

DAY 5

Literature for Week 2

Different texts for different purposes

Counting Noodles

Teacher Read Aloud

Purposes

- oral language
- listening strategy
- comprehension skill

Big Books:

Higglety Pigglety: A Book of Rhymes

Purposes

- oral language development
- phonemic awareness

From Apples to Zebras: A Book of ABC's

Purposes

- alphabet recognition
- letters and sounds

Ten Little Puppies

A Song from the Oral Hispanic Tradition

adapted by Elena Vázquez

illustrated by Scott Nash

Big Book: Main Selection

Purposes

- concepts of print
- reading strategy
- story language
- comprehension skill

Also available in Little Big Book and audiotape

Also in the Big Book:
- Art Link

Purposes

- reading strategies
- comprehension skills
- concepts of print

Phonics Library

Also available in Take-Home version

Purpose

- applying phonics skills and high-frequency words

Leveled Books

On My Way Paperback

Nan Can!
by Demaris Tyler
page T153

Little Readers for Guided Reading
Collection K

Houghton Mifflin Classroom Bookshelf
Level K

Technology

www.eduplace.com
Log on to *Education Place* for more activities relating to *Let's Count!*

www.bookadventure.org
This free Internet reading incentive program provides thousands of titles for students to read.

Instructional Goals

Learning to Read

- ✓ *Phonemic Awareness:* Blending Onset and Rime
- *Strategy Focus:* Summarize
- ✓ *Comprehension Skill:* Story Structure: Beginning, Middle, End
- ✓ *Phonics Skills*
- *Phonemic Awareness:* Beginning Sound / g /
- Initial Consonant *G, g;* Short *a + n*
- *Compare and Review:* Initial Consonants: *g, v, p*
- ✓ *High-Frequency Word:* go
- ✓ *Concepts of Print:* Letter and Word, First / Last Letter in a Word

Word Work

- *High-Frequency Word Practice:* Word Families: *-an, -at*

Writing & Language

- *Vocabulary Skills:* Rhyming Words, Using Naming Words
- *Writing Skills:* Writing a Number Rhyme, Writing a Poem

✓ = tested skills

Leveled Books

Have children read in appropriate levels daily.

Phonics Library
On My Way Practice Readers
Little Big Books
Houghton Mifflin Classroom Bookshelf

Day 1

Opening Routines, *T60–T61*

Word Wall
- **Phonemic Awareness:** Blending Onset and Rime

Teacher Read Aloud
Counting Noodles, T64–T65
- **Strategy:** Summarize
- **Comprehension:** Story Structure: Beginning, Middle, End

Phonics
Instruction
- Phonemic Awareness, Beginning Sound / g /, T66–T67; *Practice Book, 145–146*

High-Frequency Word Practice
- Words: *see, I, like, my, T68*

Oral Language
- Rhyming Words, *T69*
- Listening and Speaking, *T69*

Managing Small Groups
Teacher-Led Group
- Reread familiar **Phonics Library** selections

Independent Groups
- Finish *Practice Book, 143–146*
- **Phonics Center:** Theme 5, Week 2, Day 1
- Dramatic Play, Writing, Book, other Centers

Day 2

Opening Routines, *T70–T71*

Word Wall
- **Phonemic Awareness:** Blending Onset and Rime

Sharing the Big Book
Ten Little Puppies, T72–T73
- **Strategy:** Summarize
- **Comprehension:** Story Structure: Beginning, Middle, End

Phonics
Instruction, Practice
- Initial Consonant g, T74–T75
- *Practice Book, 147*

High-Frequency Word
- New Word: *go, T76–T77*
- *Practice Book, 148*

High-Frequency Word Practice
- Building Sentences, *T78*

Vocabulary Expansion
- Using Naming Words, *T79*
- Listening and Speaking, *T79*

Managing Small Groups
Teacher-Led Group
- Begin *Practice Book, 147–148* and handwriting **Blackline Masters 163 or 189.**

Independent Groups
- Finish *Practice Book, 147–148* and handwriting **Blackline Masters 163 or 189.**
- **Phonics Center:** Theme 5, Week 2, Day 2
- Math, Art, other Centers

Technology

Lesson Planner CD-ROM: Customize your planning for *Let's Count!* with the Lesson Planner.

Day 3

Opening Routines, *T80–T81*

Word Wall

- **Phonemic Awareness:** Blending Onset and Rime

Sharing the Big Book
Ten Little Puppies, T82–T85
- **Strategy:** Summarize
- **Comprehension:** Story Structure: Beginning, Middle, End, *T83; Practice Book, 149*
- **Concepts of Print:** Letter and Word; First/Last Letter in a Word, *T84*

Phonics
Practice, Application
- Consonant *g, T88–T89*

Instruction
- Blending *-an, T88–T89; Practice Book, 150*
- **Phonics Library:** "Go, Cat!," *T89*

Building Words
- Word Family: *-an, T90*

✎ **Shared Writing**
- Writing a Number Rhyme, *T91*

Managing Small Groups
Teacher-Led Group
- Read **Phonics Library** selection "Go, Cat!"
- Write letters *A, a;* begin **Blackline Masters 157 or 183.**
- Begin *Practice Book, 149–150*

Independent Groups
- Finish **Blackline Masters 157 or 183** and *Practice Book, 149–150.*
- Art, Math, other Centers

Day 4

Opening Routines, *T92–T93*

Word Wall

- **Phonemic Awareness:** Blending Onset and Rime

Sharing the Big Book
Art Link: "Meet Scott Nash," *T94–T95*
- **Strategy:** Summarize
- **Comprehension:** Story Structure: Beginning, Middle, End
- **Concepts of Print:** Return Sweep; First/Last Letter in a Word

Phonics
Practice
- Blending *-an* Words, *T96–T97; Practice Book, 151*

Building Words
- Word Families: *-an, -at, T98*

✎ **Interactive Writing**
- Writing a Poem, *T99*

Managing Small Groups
Teacher-Led Group
- Reread **Phonics Library** selection "Go, Cat!," *T95*
- Begin *Practice Book, 151*

Independent Groups
- Finish *Practice Book, 151*
- **Phonics Center:** Theme 5, Week 2, Day 4
- Writing, other Centers

Day 5

Opening Routines, *T100–T101*

Word Wall

- **Phonemic Awareness:** Blending Onset and Rime

Revisiting the Literature
- **Comprehension:** Story Structure: Beginning, Middle, End, *T102*

Building Fluency
- **Phonics Library:** "Go, Cat!," *T103*

Phonics
Review
- Familiar Consonants; *-an, -at, T104*

High-Frequency Word Review
- Words: *I, see, my, like, a, to, and, go, T105; Practice Book, 152*

Building Words
- Word Families: *-an, -at, T106*

✎ **Independent Writing**
- Journals: Recording Information, *T107*

Managing Small Groups
Teacher-Led Group
- Reread familiar **Phonics Library** selections
- Begin *Practice Book, 152,* **Blackline Master 36.**

Independent Groups
- Reread **Phonics Library** selections
- Finish *Practice Book, 152,* **Blackline Master 36.**
- Centers

Setting up the Centers

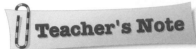

Make a counting chart using beans and a plastic photo album sleeve. Place the chart in the Math Center.

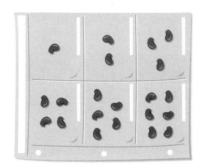

Phonics Center

Materials • Phonics Center materials for Theme 5, Week 2

Pairs work together to sort Picture cards by initial sound and build words using this week's letter and the -an word family. See pages T67, T75, and T97 for this week's Phonics Center activities.

Writing Center

Materials • number rhyme charts from Days 2 and 3 • paper • crayons or markers

Children write and illustrate a sentence from one of the number rhyme charts. See page T99 for this week's Writing Center activity.

I see 1, 1 cat plays in the sun.

I see 2, 2 cats stuck in glue.

Math Center

Materials • buttons • cups labeled 1 to 10 • counters
• Blackline Masters 80–87

Partners count buttons and place them in cups labeled
1 to 10. They also use a 2-part sorting mat to make
different combinations of numbers 3 through 10. See
pages T73 and T87 for this week's Math Center activities.

Dramatic Play Center

Materials • doll

Small groups dramatize the story *Counting Noodles* while others
are the audience. The audience helps the father count aloud.
See page T63 for this week's Dramatic Play Center activity.

Art Center

Materials • drawing paper • markers • paper lunch bags

Children draw pictures of different kinds of dogs. They also make
paper bag puppy puppets. See pages T79 and T87 for this week's
Art Center activities.

Day at a Glance

Learning to Read

Teacher Read Aloud:

Counting Noodles

☑ **Learning About / g /,** *page T66*

Word Work

High-Frequency Word Practice, *page T68*

Writing & Language

Oral Language, *page T69*

 Half-Day Kindergarten

☑ Indicates lessons for tested skills. Choose additional activities as time allows.

Opening

Calendar

Sunday	Monday	Tuesday	Wednesday	Thursday	Friday	Saturday
			1	2	3	4
5	6	7	8	9	10	11
12	13	14	15	16	17	18
19	20	21	22	23	24	25
26	27	28	29	30	31	

Put a new twist on counting: *Today is (name the month and date). What date was it three days ago? What will the date be two days from now?*

1 2 3

Daily Message

Modeled Writing After writing the message, tell children that the family in the story likes to count things. Call on volunteers to count the letters in words you frame. Have others count the words in the sentence and name the first and last letters in several words.

> Today we'll hear a silly story about a very silly family.

Have children take turns reading Word Wall words as you call them out. Ask others to count the letters in each word.

Routines

Daily Phonemic Awareness
Blending Onset and Rime

- Read "One, Two, Three, Four, Five" on page 22 of *Higglety Pigglety.*

- Play a guessing game. *I'll say some sounds. You put the sounds together to make words from the poem.* /f/ /ive/ (five); /s/ /ix/ (six)

- Continue with other one-syllable words from the poem.

- For children who need more practice, add these words: *ten, tip, pan, let, bat, for, go, sat, sun, fog.*

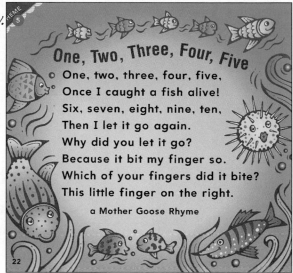

One, Two, Three, Four, Five

One, two, three, four, five,
Once I caught a fish alive!
Six, seven, eight, nine, ten,
Then I let it go again.
Why did you let it go?
Because it bit my finger so.
Which of your fingers did it bite?
This little finger on the right.

a Mother Goose Rhyme

Higglety Pigglety: A Book of Rhymes, page 22

Getting Ready to Learn

To help plan their day, tell children that they will

- listen to a story called *Counting Noodles.*

- meet a new Alphafriend, Gertie Goose.

- act out the story in the Dramatic Play Center.

Opening Routines   T61

Read Aloud

Purposes • oral language • listening strategy
• comprehension skill

Selection Summary
A family of noodleheads find their afternoon ruined when the father, determines that one family member is missing.

Key Concept
Counting

 English Language Learners

Most children will have eaten some type of noodle, though they may not know the word *noodle*. Share with children a variety of noodles, including pasta, egg noodles, and those eaten in Asian countries. Introduce the word *noodle*, and have children repeat it after you. Ask: *Do you eat noodles? Which kind of noodles do you like?*

Teacher Read Aloud
Oral Language/Comprehension

▶ **Building Background**

Call on four children to come to the front of the room. Ask each child in the group to count how many children you called up. Repeat with different numbers of children until all children have had a chance to be in a group and count the group members. Tell children that they are going to hear a story called *Counting Noodles.* It is about a family, called the Noodles, who like to count things.

Strategy: Summarize

Teacher Modeling Tell children that good readers summarize or retell a story to better understand and remember it.

Think Aloud

When I retell a story, I tell in my own words about the important things. I'll tell where the story took place, who was in the story, and all the important things that happened. As I read, I'll remember these things.

 Comprehension Focus:
Story Structure: Beginning, Middle, End

Teacher Modeling Tell children that good readers and listeners think about the order in which things in a story take place.

Think Aloud

As I read, I will think about what happens at the beginning, in the middle, and at the end of the story. This will help me tell what the story is about.

▶ Listening to the Story

Read the story, exaggerating the dialogue to show how silly the Noodles are. Note that the Read Aloud art is also available on the back of the Theme Poster.

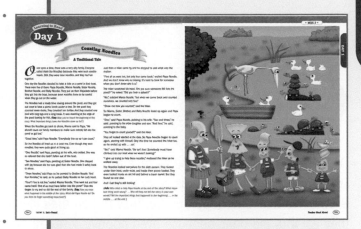

▶ Responding

Summarizing the Story Help children summarize parts of the story.

- *Who are the Noodles? What happened at the beginning of the story?*

- *What happened in the middle? Why did the Noodles think that one of the family members had fallen into the pond?*

- *What happened at the end? Why couldn't the Noodles find the missing person?*

- *What did you like best about the story?*

Practice Book pages 143–144 Children will complete the pages during small group time.

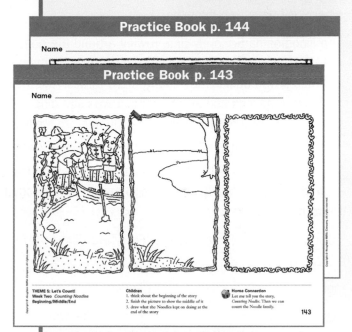

Practice Book p. 144

Practice Book p. 143

At Group Time

Dramatic Play Center

Have children work together in groups of five to re-enact the story. Children pick roles for the father, mother, sister, brother, and hiker. They use a doll to play the role of the baby.

Teacher's Note

Many countries share the tradition of "noodle" tales, silly stories about people or families. While many of these tales have been told for generations, you may wish to share more contemporary favorites such as the *Amelia Bedelia* books by Peggy Parish.

Counting Noodles

A Traditional Tale

Once upon a time, there was a very silly family. Everyone called them the Noodles because they were such noodle-heads. Still, they were nice noodles, and they had fun together.

One day the Noodles decided to take a ride on a pond in their boat. There were five of them: Papa Noodle, Mama Noodle, Sister Noodle, Brother Noodle, and Baby Noodle. They put on their lifejackets before they got into the boat, because even noodles know to be careful when they go out on the water.

The Noodles had a lovely time rowing around the pond, and they got out once to have a picnic lunch under a tree. On the pond they counted seven ducks. They counted ten turtles. And they counted one bird with long legs and a long beak. It was standing at the edge of the pond looking for fish. (**Say:** *Now you've heard the beginning of this story. What important things have the Noodles done so far?*)

When the Noodles got back to shore, Mama said to Papa, "We should count our family members to make sure nobody fell into the pond or got lost."

"Good idea," said Papa Noodle. "Everybody line up so I can count."

So the Noodles all lined up in a neat row. Even though they were noodles, they were quite good at lining up.

"One Noodle," said Papa, pointing at his wife, who smiled. She was so relieved that she hadn't fallen out of the boat.

"Two Noodles," said Papa, pointing at Sister Noodle. She clapped with joy because she too was glad that she had made it safely back to shore.

"Three Noodles," said Papa as he pointed to Brother Noodle. "And four Noodles," he said, as he patted Baby Noodle on her curly head.

"Four? Four is not five," wailed Mama Noodle. "Five went out and four came back! One of us must have fallen into the pond!" Then she began to cry, and so did the rest of the family. (**Say:** *Now you know what happened in the middle of the story. What did Papa Noodle do? Do you think he forgot something important?*)

Just then a hiker came by, and he stopped to ask what was the matter.

"Five of us went out, but only four came back," wailed Papa Noodle. And we don't know who is missing. It's hard to look for someone when you don't know who it is."

The hiker scratched his head. "Are you sure someone fell into the pond?" he asked. "Did you hear a splash?"

"No," sobbed Mama Noodle, "but when we came back and counted ourselves, we counted only four."

"Show me how you counted," said the hiker.

So Mama, Sister, Brother, and Baby Noodle lined up again and Papa began to count.

"One," said Papa Noodle, pointing to his wife. "Two and three," he said, pointing to his older daughter and son. "And four," he said, pointing to the baby.

"You forgot to count yourself!" said the hiker.

They all looked startled at the idea. So Papa Noodle began to count again, starting with himself. Only *this* time he counted the hiker too, so he ended up with . . . *six*!

"Six!" said Mama Noodle. "Six isn't five! Somebody must have climbed into our boat when we weren't looking!"

"I give up trying to help these noodles," muttered the hiker as he walked away.

The Noodles looked everywhere for the sixth person. They looked under their boat, under rocks, and inside their picnic basket. They even looked inside an ant hill and behind a trash barrel. But they found no one else.

And I bet they're still looking!

(**Ask:** *Who tried to help Papa Noodle at the end of the story? What important thing went wrong? . . . Who will help me tell the story in your own words? Tell the important things that happened in the beginning . . . in the middle . . . at the end.*)

Day 1

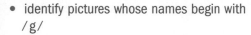
Children

- identify pictures whose names begin with /g/

MATERIALS

- **Alphafriend Cards** *Gertie Goose, Pippa Pig, Vinny Volcano*
- **Alphafriend Audiotape** Theme 5
- **Alphafolder** *Gertie Goose*
- **Picture Cards** for *g, p, v*
- **Phonics Center:** Theme 5, Week 2, Day 1

Home Connection

A take-home version of Gertie Goose's song is on an **Alphafriends Blackline Master.** Children can share the song with their families.

English Language Learners

Most children will be able to produce /g/. However, they may need to preview words in Gertie's song. Show pictures of a garden gate, a crate, a goat, and a gopher. Pantomime how to "gobble up" something. If possible, play a recording of "Jingle Bells" to familarize them with the tune.

Phonemic Awareness

✓ Beginning Sound

▶ Introducing the Alphafriend: Gertie Goose

Use the Alphafriend routine to introduce Gertie Goose.

1 **Alphafriend Riddle** Read these clues emphasizing the /g/ sound slightly:

- ■ *This Alphafriend is an animal. Her sound is /g/. Say it with me: /g/.*
- ■ *This bird looks a little like a duck, but she's bigger.*
- ■ *When she's with her friends, she is part of a gaggle of geese.*

When most hands are up, call on children until they guess *goose*.

2 **Pocket Chart** Display Gertie Goose in a pocket chart. Say her name, stretching the /g/ sound slightly, and have children echo this.

3 **Alphafriend Audiotape** Play Gertie Goose's song. *Listen for words that start with /g/.*

4 **Alphafolder** Have children name the /g/ pictures in the illustration.

5 **Summarize**

- ■ *What is our Alphafriend's name? What is her sound?*
- ■ *What words in our Alphafriend's song start with /g/?*
- ■ *Each time you look at Gertie Goose this week, remember the /g/ sound.*

Gertie Goose's Song

(Tune: "Jingle Bells")

Gertie Goose, Gertie Goose,
Guards the garden gate
So goat can't come and
 gobble up
The goodies in her crate.

▶ Listening for / g /

Compare and Review: / v /, / p / Display Alphafriends *Vinny Volcano* and *Pippa Pig* opposite *Gertie Goose*. Review each character's sound.

Hold up Picture Cards one at a time. Tell children you'll name some pictures, and they should signal "thumbs up" for each one that begins like Gertie's name. Volunteers put the cards below Gertie's picture. For "thumbs down" words, volunteers put cards below the correct Alphafriends.

Pictures: *game, peach, goat, van, pot, girl, purse, vase, gate, vest*

Tell children they will sort more pictures in the Phonics Center today.

▶ Apply

Practice Book pages 145–146 Children will complete the pages at small group time.

At Group Time
Phonics Center

Use the Phonics Center materials for **Theme 5, Week 2, Day 1**.

Day 1

High-Frequency Word Practice

▶ **Matching Words**

OBJECTIVES

Children

- read high-frequency words
- create and write sentences with high-frequency words

MATERIALS

- **Word Cards** *I, like, my, see*
- ***Higglety Pigglety: A Book of Rhymes,*** page 6
- **Picture Cards** *dog, run*
- **Punctuation Card:** period

Teacher's Note

Make a word card for *can* before this lesson.

■ Display Word Cards for the high-frequency words *I, like, my, see,* in a pocket chart. Call on children to identify each word and to match it on the Word Wall.

■ Remind children that these are words they often see in books. *I'll read a poem. You listen to hear if these words are in it.*

■ Read "Everybody Says" on page 6 of *Higglety Pigglety. Did you hear some of these words in the poem? Let's match the Word Cards to the words in the poem.* Children will match *I, like,* and *my.*

Everybody Says

Everybody says
I look just like my mother.
Everybody says
I'm the image of Aunt Bee.
Everybody says
My nose is like my father's.
But I want to look like ME!

by Dorothy Aldis

6

***Higglety Pigglety: A Book of Rhymes,* page 6**

Writing Opportunity Have children use the Word Cards from the activity above, along with a Word Card for *can* and the Picture Cards, to make sentences. Children can write and illustrate one of the sentences or use the words to create their own sentences with rebus pictures. Allow temporary phonics spellings for words children choose.

Oral Language

▶ Rhyming Words

Listening and Speaking Talk about rhyming words. Explain that rhyming words end with the same sounds. Give some examples: *a sheep in a jeep; a fuss on the bus; a bee on your knee.* Tell children that they can make a rhyme, too. Display the following Picture Cards: *boat, box, cat, dog, fox, goat, hat, log.*

■ Call on a child to choose a card and say its picture name. Have another child find the card that rhymes.

■ Place rhyming pairs in a pocket chart. Then help children brainstorm rhyming phrases for the words. Record their suggestions on chart paper. Invite children to add other rhyming pairs to the chart.

At Group Time
Writing Center

Materials • drawing paper • markers

Put the chart from above in the Writing Center. Children can refer to the pictures and use their knowledge of rhyme to help them to illustrate a rhyme of their choosing. Some children will be able to write the rhymes on their pictures.

Fox in a box.

Children
• use rhyming words

MATERIALS

Picture Cards *boat, box, cat, dog, fox, goat, hat, log*

Portfolio Opportunity
Save children's rhymes for their portfolios.

English Language Learners

Make sure children know the names for the Picture Cards. Help them to name each picture using a complete sentence: "It's a _____" or "That's a _____." Check for the pronunciation of the /ks/ in *box* and *fox.* Help children say all the words and find the pairs that rhyme.

Day 2

Day at a Glance

Learning to Read

Big Book:

Ten Little Puppies

☑ **Phonics:**
Initial Consonant g,
page T74

☑ **High-Frequency Word:** *go,*
page T76

Word Work

High-Frequency Word Practice,
page T78

Writing & Language

Vocabulary Expansion, *page T79*

 Half-Day Kindergarten

☑ Indicates lessons for tested skills. Choose additional activities as time allows.

Opening

Calendar

Sunday	Monday	Tuesday	Wednesday	Thursday	Friday	Saturday
			1	2	3	4
5	6	7	8	9	10	11
12	13	14	15	16	17	18
19	20	21	22	23	24	25
26	27	28	29	30	31	

Discuss how the weather changes from season to season. To compare the seasons, talk about the clothes children wear during the different seasons.

Daily Message

Modeled Writing Use some *g* words in today's message. Point them out as you read.

> Mrs. Graham will play a guitar in music class.

Today, children can take turns reading Word Wall words as you call them out. Choose children who need practice with these words.

Routines

✓ Daily Phonemic Awareness
Blending Onset and Rime

- Display Picture Cards *bell, bug, goat,* and *hat.*

- Say: *I'll say some sounds. You put them together to make words that name the pictures. Listen:/ g / / oat /. Who can show me the picture whose name has the sounds / g / / oat /? That's right, goat. Say the sounds with me / g / / oat /, goat.*

- Continue with the other Picture Cards.

- If needed, add these words: *cut, let, cup, jig, wag, tap, tug, fun.*

Getting Ready to Learn

To help plan their day, tell children that they will

- listen to a Big Book: *Ten Little Puppies.*

- learn the new letters *G* and *g,* and sort words that begin with *g.*

- count items from 1 to 10 in the Math Center.

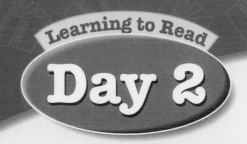

Big Book

Ten Little Puppies
A Song from the Oral Hispanic Tradition

adapted by Elena Vázquez
illustrated by Scott Nash

Purposes • concepts of print • story language • reading strategy • comprehension skill

---

Selection Summary

In this traditional counting song, a boy with ten puppies is left with none as they depart one by one. The story doesn't end there, however; ten more puppies arrive to keep the boy company!

Key Concepts

Counting
Rhyming words

English Language Learners

Count from one to ten with children. Then help children to count back from ten. Listen for how children pronounce *three*. As needed, model where to put the tongue to produce the sound for *thr*.

Sharing the Big Book
Oral Language/Comprehension

▶ Building Background

Read aloud the title of the Big Book. Tell children that this story is a counting song. Discuss what children know about counting songs. Encourage them to share counting songs or rhymes they know, such as "One Potato, Two Potato" or "This Old Man."

Strategy: Summarize

Teacher Modeling Model the Summarize strategy as you read the title again.

> #### Think Aloud
>
> *When I finish reading* Ten Little Puppies, *I will want to retell the story. So as I read, I will think about who is in the story and the important things that happen.*

✓ Comprehension Focus:
Story Structure: Beginning, Middle, End

Teacher Modeling Tell children that good readers and listeners think about what happens in the story.

> #### Think Aloud
>
> *As I read, I will think about what happens at the beginning of the story, in the middle, and at the end. This will help me remember the story.*

▶ Sharing the Story

Read the selection aloud, emphasizing the rhythm and rhyme. Track the print with a pointer or your finger as you read. As you read, pause for children to supply the rhyming number word.

▶ Responding

Personal Response Encourage children to use their knowledge of numbers and rhyme to remember and retell the story.

- *Did the boy like his puppies? How do you know?*

- *How do numbers and rhyming words help you remember the story?*

- *Which puppy was your favorite? Why?*

- *What do you think will happen to the ten new puppies?*

At Group Time

±= Math Center

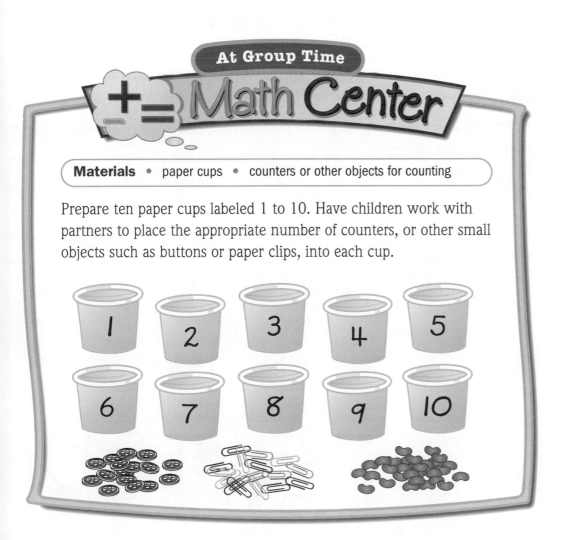

Materials • paper cups • counters or other objects for counting

Prepare ten paper cups labeled 1 to 10. Have children work with partners to place the appropriate number of counters, or other small objects such as buttons or paper clips, into each cup.

Extra Support

MEETING INDIVIDUAL NEEDS

Some children may benefit from using the pictures to retell the story. They can count the remaining puppies to see that there is one fewer on each spread. Or they can use picture clues to recall the rhymes.

Sharing the Big Book T73

OBJECTIVES

Children

- identify words that begin with /g/
- identify pictures whose names begin with /g/
- form the letters G, g

MATERIALS

- **Alphafriend Card** *Gertie Goose*
- **Letter Cards** *g, p, v*
- **Picture Cards** for *g, p, v*
- **Blackline Master 163**
- **Phonics Center:** Theme 5, Week 2, Day 2

 Extra Support

To help children remember the sound for *g*, provide a phrase that incorporates the target sound such as, *"Good job."*

Phonics

Initial Consonant g

▶ Develop Phonemic Awareness

Beginning Sound Demonstrate how to make a goose bill with your hand. Then read the lyrics of Gertie Goose's song, and have children echo you line-for-line. Have them listen for the /g/ words and open and close their "goose bills" for each one.

> **Gertie Goose's Song**
>
> Gertie Goose, Gertie Goose,
> Guards the garden gate.
> So goat and gopher don't come in
> To gobble what's in her crate.

▶ Connect Sounds to Letters

Beginning Letter Display the *Gertie Goose* card, and have children name the letter on the picture. Say: *The letter g stands for the sound /g/, as in goose. When you see a g, remember Gertie Goose. That will help you remember the sound /g/.*

Write *goose* on the board. Underline the *g*. **What is the first letter in the word goose?** (g) **Goose starts with /g/, so g is the first letter I write for goose.**

Compare and Review: g, v, p In a pocket chart, display the Letter Cards as shown and the Picture Cards in random order. Review the sounds for *g, v,* and *p*. In turn, children can name a picture, say the beginning sound, and put the cards below the right letter.

Tell children that they will sort more pictures in the Phonics Center today.

▶ Handwriting

Writing G, g Tell children that now they'll learn to *write* the letters that stand for /g/: capital *G* and small *g*. Write each letter as you recite the handwriting rhyme. Children can chant each rhyme as they "write" the letter in the air.

Handwriting Rhyme: G

Start at the top and curve left like a capital C. Add a short line in the middle to make capital G.

Handwriting Rhyme: g

Make a small circle in the middle, just a little hoop. Go straight down by the circle and end with a scoop.

▶ Apply

Practice Book page 147 Children will complete this page at small group time.

Blackline Master 163 This page provides additional handwriting practice.

At Group Time

Phonics Center

Use the Phonics Center materials for **Theme 5, Week 2, Day 2**.

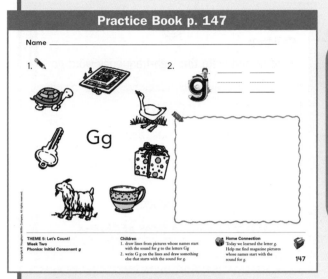
Practice Book p. 147

Name _____

THEME 5: Let's Count!
Week Two
Phonics: Initial Consonant *g*

Children
1. draw lines from pictures whose names start with the sound for *g* to the letters Gg
2. write G g on the lines and draw something else that starts with the sound for g.

Home Connection
Today we learned the letter *g*. Help me find magazine pictures whose names start with the sound for g.

147

Teacher's Note

Handwriting practice for the continuous stroke style is available on **Blackline Master 189.**

Portfolio Opportunity

Children may wish to save their hand-writing samples in their portfolios.

OBJECTIVES

Children

- read and write the high-frequency word *go*

MATERIALS

- **Word Cards** *I, a, to, see, and, go*
- **Picture Cards** *cat, cow, dog, farm, goat, hen, horse, pig*
- **Punctuation Card:** period
- *Higglety Pigglety: A Book of Rhymes,* page 30

 # High-Frequency Word

New Word: go

▶ **Teach**

Tell children that they'll learn to read and write a word that they use when they speak and that they will often see in books. Say *go* and use it in context.

We *go* to school.   A car can *go* fast.   A boat can *go* in the water.

Write *go* on the board, and have children spell it as you point to the letters. Say: **Spell go with me, g-o, go.** Then lead children in a chant, clapping on each beat, to help them remember the spelling: *g-o, go! g-o, go!*

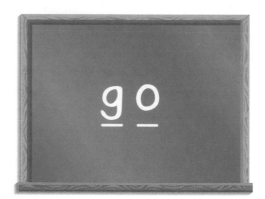

Word Wall   Post *go* on the Word Wall, and remind children to look there when they need to remember how to write the word.

▶ **Practice**

Reading Build the following sentences in a pocket chart. Children take turns reading the sentences. Leave the pocket chart out, along with additional Picture Cards, so that children can practice building and reading their own sentences.

Display *Higglety Pigglety: A Book of Rhymes*, page 30.

- Share the rhyme "Stop and Go."

- Reread the title, tracking the print. Have children point to the word *go*.

- Read the line: "The red means STOP, the green means GO!" Have children point to GO. If children have difficulty locating the word, point to it and spell it with them. Ask them what they notice. (capital letters)

Higglety Pigglety: A Book of Rhymes, page 30

▶ Apply

Practice Book page 148 Children will read and write *go* as they complete the Practice Book page. They will practice reading *go* in the **Phonics Library** story "Go, Cat!"

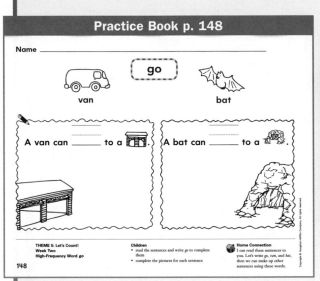

Practice Book p. 148

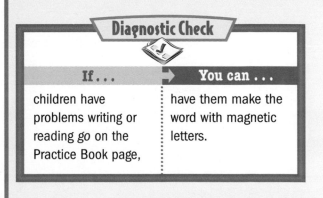

If...	You can...
children have problems writing or reading *go* on the Practice Book page,	have them make the word with magnetic letters.

High-Frequency Word (T77)

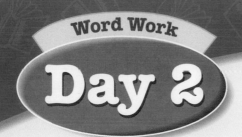

Day 2

OBJECTIVES

Children

- read high-frequency words
- create and write sentences with high-frequency words

MATERIALS

- **Word Cards** *l, go, to, a*
- **Picture Cards** *farm, zoo*
- **Punctuation Card:** period

Teacher's Note

For this activity, you will also need to make a word card for *can*.

High-Frequency Word Practice

▶ Building Sentences

Tell children that you want to build a sentence about a place where people can go.

- Display the Word Cards and Picture Cards in random order. Put the Word Card *I* in a pocket chart, and read it.

- *I want the next word to be* can. *Who can find that word? That's right! This word is* can. *Now who can read my sentence so far?*

- Continue building the sentence *I can go to a _____.* Children choose the Picture Card for the blank.

- Read the sentence with children.

 **Writing Opportunity** Have children write the sentence and illustrate it. Remind them that if they want to add a word of their own, they can write it by saying the word slowly and writing the letters they hear.

Vocabulary Expansion

▶ **Using Naming Words**

Listening and Speaking Look through *Ten Little Puppies.* Ask children if they can name a kind, or *breed,* of dog they see. Brainstorm a list of dog breeds with children. Record the list on chart paper.

Then ask children to help you think of a good title for the list. Ask: ***What should we call this list? Remember, a good title tells what the writing is about.***

Kinds of Dogs

golden retriever
poodle
dalmation
German shepherd
cocker spaniel

At Group Time
Art Center

Materials • drawing paper • markers or crayons

Have children choose a favorite type of dog to illustrate and tell why it is their favorite. Some children may add color words when they label their drawings.

DAY 2

English Language Learners

Both English language learners and English-speaking classmates can benefit from looking through books about breeds of dogs. Ask children to find dogs they have seen before. As needed, help them to name the different breeds. Encourage children to talk about each dog's characteristics.

Day at a Glance

Learning to Read

Big Book:

Ten Little Puppies

✓ **Phonics: Blending -an Words,** *page T88*

Word Work

Building Words, *page T90*

Writing & Language

Shared Writing, *page T91*

☀ **Half-Day Kindergarten**

✓ Indicates lessons for tested skills. Choose additional activities as time allows.

Opening

Calendar

Sunday	Monday	Tuesday	Wednesday	Thursday	Friday	Saturday
			1	2	3	4
5	6	7	8	9	10	11
12	13	14	15	16	17	18
19	20	21	22	23	24	25
26	27	28	29	30	31	

Discuss weekend plans with children. Count how many days until the weekend and until the class meets again for school.

Daily Message

Modeled Writing Try to use words starting with previously taught initial consonant sounds in the daily message. Call on volunteers to point to and circle each target sound.

We will count buttons at the Math Center.

Choose a child to point to and read the new word that was added to the wall this week, *go.* **Compare** go *with the other words. What do you notice?*
(*Go* has two letters like *an, at, is,* and *to; go* has an *o* like *to.*)

Routines

 ## Daily Phonemic Awareness

Blending Onset and Rime

- Read "One, Two, Three, Four, Five" on page 22 of *Higglety Pigglety.*

- Play a blending game using words from the poem. *I'll say some sounds. You put them together to make words:* /f/ /ish/ (fish); /g/ /ō/ (go); /r/ /ight/ (right); /s/ /ix/ (six); /n/ /ine/ (nine).

- Continue with other one-syllable words: *pen, pat, not, fig, lap, pal, get, sad, log.*

- Monitor children's blending to make sure they are blending correctly. If they are not, model blending carefully.

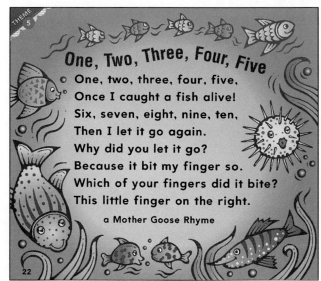

Higglety Pigglety: A Book of Rhymes, page 22

Getting Ready to Learn

To help plan their day, tell children that they will

- reread and talk about the Big Book: *Ten Little Puppies.*

- read a story called "Go, Cat!"

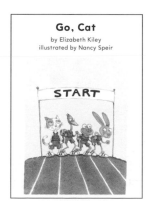

- explore counting and regrouping numbers in the Math Center.

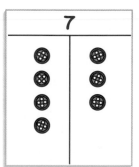

Sharing the Big Book

OBJECTIVES

Children

- identify beginning, middle, and end of a story
- distinguish between letter and word
- identify the first and last letters of a word

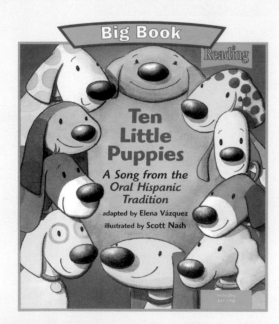

Big Book

Reading

Ten Little Puppies

A Song from the Oral Hispanic Tradition

adapted by Elena Vázquez
illustrated by Scott Nash

Reading for Understanding Reread the story, emphasizing the rhythm and rhyme. Pause for Supporting Comprehension points.

 Extra Support

Some children may have trouble connecting numbers to their corresponding values. Help them match counters to the remaining dogs on each spread to provide a concrete example of the number.

I had ten little puppies.

1

page 1

One of the ten went out to dine.

2

Now there are only nine, nine, nine.

3

pages 2–3

One of the nine stayed up too late.

4

Now there are only eight, eight, eight.

5

pages 4–5

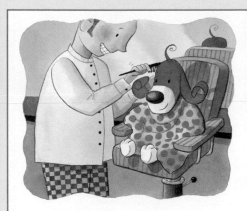

One of the eight
got a trim at eleven.

6

Now there are only
seven, seven, seven.

7

pages 6–7

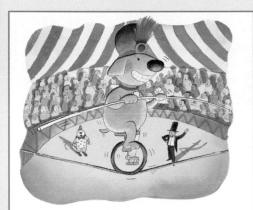

One of the seven
tried some new tricks.

8

Now there are only
six, six, six.

9

pages 8–9

One of the six
learned how to drive.

10

Now there are only
five, five, five.

11

pages 10–11

▶ Supporting Comprehension

page 1

✓ Comprehension Focus: Story Structure: Beginning, Middle, End

Teacher-Student Modeling *Good readers think about what happens in a story. This is a special counting book, so we go from ten to zero in order. What do we know about the boy and the puppies at the beginning of the story?*

pages 2–5

Fantasy/Realism

■ *Could the things in this story really happen?*

(No. Real dogs don't dine out or stay up watching TV.)

pages 9–11

Strategy: Summarize

Teacher-Student Modeling Review that good readers think about what happens to retell a story. Prompt:

■ *What has happened in the story so far?*

Oral Language

On a rereading, note interesting words.

dine: To dine means to eat.

trim: A trim is a haircut. Just a bit of hair is cut when you have a trim.

DAY 3

Sharing the Big Book (T83)

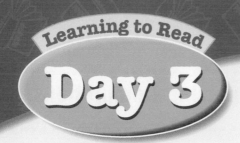

▶ Supporting Comprehension

pages 12–13

Making Predictions

■ *What do you think will happen next?* (One more puppy will leave.) *Which one do you think it will be?* (Children may point to the yellow dog walking off at the top of the picture.)

pages 14–17

Noting Details

■ Read pages 14–15. *Now look at page 16. Is this the dog you thought would leave? Now look at page 17. Which dog will leave next?*

Revisiting the Text

pages 16–17

Concepts of Print

 Letter and Word; First/Last Letter in a Word

■ *How many words are on page 16?* (10) Choose a child to frame the first word. Then frame the word *bed* and read it aloud. *How many letters are in this word? What is the first letter? The last letter?* Repeat with the word *now*.

One of the five
moved in next door.

12

Now there are only
four, four, four.

13

pages 12–13

One of the four
sailed off to sea.

14

Now there are only
three, three, three.

15

pages 14–15

One of the three
went to bed with the flu.

16

Now there are only
two, two, two.

17

pages 16–17

One of the two
went out for a run.

18

Now there is only
one, one, one.

19

pages 18–19

The one that was left
went looking for fun.

20

Now I am left with
none, none, none.

21

pages 20–21

I hear a noise.
Quick, get the door!

22

Puppies! Someone
has left me ten more!

23

pages 22–23

▶ Supporting Comprehension

pages 20–21

Cause and Effect

■ *How does the boy feel now that all the puppies are gone? Why does he feel that way?*

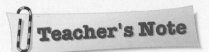
pages 22–23

✓ Comprehension Focus: Story Structure: Beginning, Middle, End

Student Modeling Have children tell what
happened at the end of the story.

Strategy: Summarizing

Student Modeling As children retell the story
in their discussion groups, have them focus on
the beginning, middle, and end.

DAY 3

📎 Teacher's Note

Language Patterns

Rhyme This story contains a strong rhyme
scheme. On a rereading, point out the words that
rhyme with the number words.

 MEETING INDIVIDUAL NEEDS **Challenge**

Have children tell what will happen to the next ten
puppies. Remind them that this is a make-believe
story, and their story can be, too.

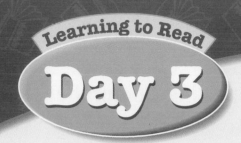

Practice Book p. 149

Name _____

Children
1. count the puppies and draw more to show how many the boy had at the beginning
2. draw what one of the puppies did in the middle of the story

Home Connection
Let me tell you the story *Ten Little Puppies*. Then I'll tell you about the pictures.

149

▶ Responding to the Story

Retelling Using pictures and these prompts, help children summarize the story:

- *How many puppies did the boy have at the beginning of the story?*

- *How did the boy end up with only nine puppies?* (One went out to dine.) **eight puppies?** (One stayed up too late.)

- *How does the rhyme help you remember more about the story?*

- *What happened at the end of the story?*

- *What part of the story was your favorite?*

Literature Circle Have small groups discuss their favorite parts of the story. *Which reason for leaving was the funniest? Which illustration was the best? Why?*

Practice Book page 149 Children complete the page at small group time.

At Group Time
Art Center

Materials • paper lunch bags • crayons or markers

Each child can make a paper bag puppet of a favorite puppy from the story. Small groups can use the puppets to role play their favorite parts of the story.

Diagnostic Check

If...	You can...
children need more practice in identifying beginning, middle, and end of stories,	have them act out the parts. Give actors cards that say "first," "then," and "at last."

At Group Time

± = Math Center

Materials • sorting mats • buttons • Blackline Masters 80–87

Make copies of **Blackline Masters 80-87** for the Math Center.
Children place the appropriate number of buttons on each work-mat. Working with partners, they group and regroup the buttons to show different ways to make each numeral.

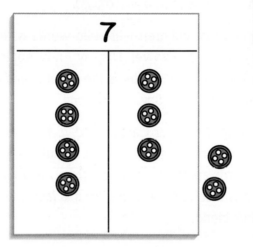

Learning to Read

Day 3

OBJECTIVES

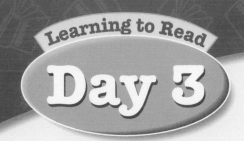

Children

- identify words with initial consonant *g*, /g/
- blend and read words with *a, c, g, m, N, o, p, r, t, v, -an*

MATERIALS

- **Alphafriend Cards** *Andy Apple, Gertie Goose, Pippa Pig, Vinny Volcano,*
- **Letter Cards** *a, c, g, m, N, n, p, r, t, v*
- **Alphafriend Audiotape** Theme 5

Practice Book p. 150

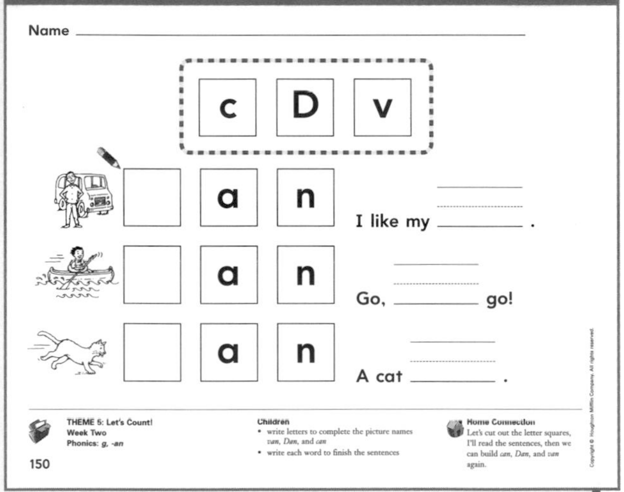

Name

| c | D | v |

| | a | n | I like my ________ .

| | a | n | Go, ________ go!

| | a | n | A cat ________ .

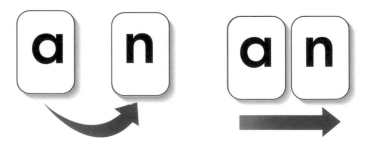

THEME 5: Let's Count!
Week Two
Phonics: *g, -an*

150

Children
- write letters to complete the picture names *van, Dan,* and *can*
- write each word to finish the sentences

Home Connection
Let's cut out the letter squares, I'll read the sentences, then we can build *can, Dan,* and *van* again.

MEETING INDIVIDUAL NEEDS — Extra Support

Ask children to listen as you say some words. Have them touch a finger to their noses and say /g/ If they hear a word that begins with /g/: *gold, garden, van, goose, pie, guitar, gone, pig, goal.*

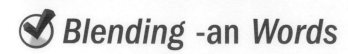

Phonics

Blending -an Words

Connect Sounds to Letters

Review Consonants *g, v, p* Play Gertie Goose's song, and have children clap for each /g/ word. Write *G* and *g* on the board, and list words from the song. Then display Alphafriends *Vinny Volcano* and *Pippa Pig* and review their sounds.

Blending Hold up Letter Card *g* and have children say /g/. Then hold up Letter Card *o*. ***This letter is a vowel ("helper letter"). Sometimes a vowel says its name. Listen as I blend these sounds.*** Model blending, as you hold the cards apart and then together: /g//ō/, *go*.

Explain that children will build words with *v* and *p*, but first they'll review a vowel. Display Andy Apple. ***You remember Andy Apple. Andy's letter is the vowel* a*, and the sound* a *usually stands for is /ă/. Say /ă/ with me.***

Hold up the Letter Cards *a* and *n*. Remind children that they know the sound for *n*. Model blending the sounds as you hold the cards apart and then together: /ă//n/, *an*. ***I've made the word* an*. The sound for* a *is first, and the sound for* n *is last.*** Have volunteers move the cards as classmates blend.

Word Wall Call on a volunteer to point to *an* on the Word Wall. Remind children that they can use *an* to make other words.

Blending *-an* Words Build *an* in a pocket chart. Then put *v* in front of *an*, and model blending /v//an/, *van*. Have children blend the sounds while you point.

Repeat with *c* to build *can*. Then blend *-an* with other known consonants to make *pan, man, Nan, ran,* and *tan*.

Practice Book page 150 Children complete the page at small group time.

Phonics in Action

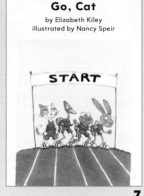
Let's Count!

Applying Phonics Skills and High-Frequency Words

Phonics Library Purposes
- apply phonics skills
- apply high-frequency words

Go, Cat
by Elizabeth Kiley
illustrated by Nancy Speir

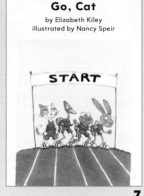

START

7

Go, Nan!
Nan ran, ran, ran.

Go, Pat!
Pat ran, ran, ran.

8   **9**

Go, Van!
Van ran, ran, ran.

Go, Cat!
Cat sat, sat, sat.

10   **11**

DAY 3

Phonics/Decoding Strategy

Teacher-Student Modeling Talk about how to use the Phonics/Decoding Strategy to read the **Phonics Library** story, "Go, Cat!"

Think Aloud

I see our new word go *in the title. The next word is* cat. *If you didn't know that word, what would you do? (blend / k / and / at / together to read* cat*) Let's read the whole title together. I think there will be a cat in this story. Let's see if I'm right.*

During a brief picture walk, encourage children to predict that they'll read about a race. Introduce the characters Nan, Pat, and Van. On page 8, choose a child to read *Nan*. Ask what Nan is doing. Write *Nan ran* on the board. Choose someone to read it. Then have children read together or silently as you coach them.

Coached Reading Have children read each page silently before reading with you. Here are some prompts to help children who need them.

page 9   *Who is the character on this page? Who will read for us?* (Pat)

page 10   *Who is this character?* (Van) Read what Van did.

page 11   *What is Cat doing? Why do you think Cat didn't run? Who will read it for us?*

Home Connection

Children can color the pictures in the take-home version of "Go, Cat!" After rereading the story on Day 4, they can take it home to read to family members.

Phonics   **T89**

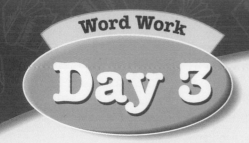

Day 3

Building Words

▶ Word Family: *-an*

Review with children that they know the sounds and letters to build the word *an*. Model how to build *an*, using the Letter Cards. ***First I'll stretch out the sounds: / ă / / n /. How many sounds do you hear? The first sound is / ă /. I'll put up a to spell that. The next sound is / n /. What letter should I choose for / n /?***

Blend / ă / and / n / and read *an*. Then ask what letter you should add to build *van*. Model how to read *van* by blending / v / with / an /.

Replace *v* with *t* and say: ***What happens if I change / v / to / t /?*** Continue making and blending *-an* words by substituting *c, m, N, p,* and *r*.

Have small groups work together to build *-an* words. Children can use sponge letters to print the words or use other manipulatives in your collection to build the words. Monitor children to make sure they can build *-an* words correctly. If they have difficulties, model building more *-an* words.

Shared Writing

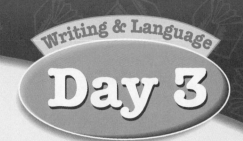

▶ Writing a Number Rhyme

Recall that the story *Ten Little Puppies* is a counting story in rhyme. Follow the shared writing routine. Have children write their own rhymes.

- **Ask:** *What rhymes with 1 (one)? Good, Carolyn can see 1 sun.*

- *What rhymes with 2? Martin has a good idea. I'll write it.*

- *Let's see how many numbers we can rhyme.*

- Have children create a predictable number rhyme chart similar to the one illustrated. Change the child's name and the numeral highlighted with each entry.

- Call on volunteers to suggest the rhyming words.

DAY 3

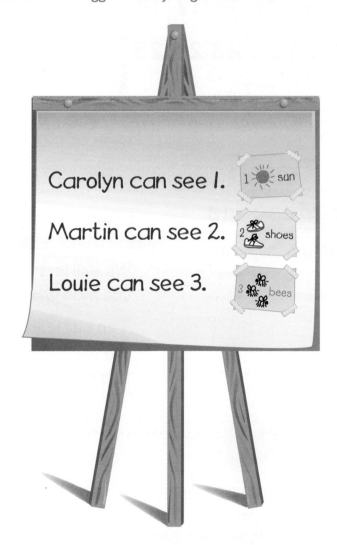

Carolyn can see 1.   1 ☀ sun

Martin can see 2.   2 👟 shoes

Louie can see 3.   3 🐝 bees

Day 4

Day at a Glance

Learning to Read

Big Book:

Meet Scott Nash

 Phonics: Reviewing /g/; Blending -an Words, *page T96*

Word Work

Building Words, *page T98*

Writing & Language

Interactive Writing, *page T99*

 Half-Day Kindergarten

 Indicates lessons for tested skills. Choose additional activities as time allows.

Opening

Calendar

Sunday	Monday	Tuesday	Wednesday	Thursday	Friday	Saturday
		1	2	3	4	
5	6	7	8	9	10	11
12	13	14	15	16	17	18
19	20	21	22	23	24	25
26						

Monday / Funday   *Tuesday / Newsday*

Review rhyming words as you complete your calendar routine. Have children suggest silly rhymes or phrases for the days of the week, for example: *Monday/ Funday, Tuesday/Newsday, Wednesday/Friendsday, Thursday/Wordsday, Friday/Myday.*

Daily Message

Modeled Writing Duplicate some of the words in the daily message. Have volunteers find the words that are the same.

> We will learn (about) the *man* who drew
>
> Ten Little Puppies. We will read (about) this *man* today.

Distribute Word Cards for the words on the Word Wall. Have children match their card to the words on the Word Wall. Then have other children chant the spelling of the word: **g-o** *spells* **go;** **a-n-d** *spells* **and.**

Routines

Daily Phonemic Awareness

Blending Onset and Rime

- Read "Going, Going, Gone" on page 25 of *Higglety Pigglety.*

- Play "Pat, Pat, Clap" to name words from the poem. Review that in "Pat, Pat, Clap" children pat for each sound you say and then clap to say the word.

- Begin with words having two sounds, such as: / g / / ō /.

- Continue with these words: / g / / ŏ / / n / (*gone*); / d / / id / (*did*); / l / / ong / (*long*).

Going, Going, Gone

Going, going, gone,
Your daddy won't be long.
Where did he go?
To shovel the snow.
Going, going, gone.

by Dennis Lee

Higglety Pigglety: A Book of Rhymes, page 25

Getting Ready to Learn

To help plan their day, tell children that they will

- read the Art Link: *Meet Scott Nash.*

- learn to make and read new words.

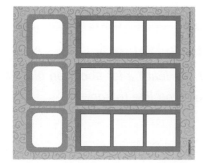

- reread a story called "Go, Cat!"

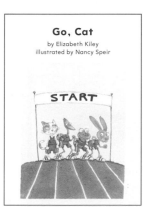

Go, Cat
by Elizabeth Kiley
illustrated by Nancy Speir

START

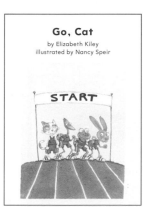

OBJECTIVES
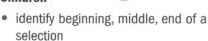

Children

- identify beginning, middle, end of a selection
- identify the first and last letter of a written word

Big Book

pages 25–31

Oral Language

studio A studio is a place where an artist works. Another kind of *studio* is a place for recording movies or music.

English Language Learners

Preview the words *artist* and *studio* with children. Tap out the syllables in each word as children say them with you. Check for correct pronunciation of *st*. As needed, work with other words that have initial or final *st* such as *stay, stairs, stop, study, start, first, fast, best, list*.

Sharing the Big Book
Art Link

▶ Building Background

Display the title page for *Meet Scott Nash* and read it aloud. ***Do you recognize this name? Where have you seen it before?*** On the cover of the Big Book, point to the illustrator's name, Scott Nash. Tell children that this article is about the man who drew the pictures for *Ten Little Puppies*. An *illustrator* is an artist.

Reading for Understanding Pause for discussion as you share the selection.

pages 26–27

Strategy: Summarize

Student Modeling Read the first two pages aloud. ***What is this selection about so far?*** (the author Scott Nash) ***How do you know?***

pages 28–29

Sequence of Events

- ***What does Scott Nash do first?*** (draw a sketch) ***What does he do next?*** (paint the picture)

page 30

Drawing Conclusions

- ***Is Scott Nash's work done when this picture is done? What more work do you think he needs to do?*** (He needs to draw more pictures for the book.)

page 31

Making Judgments

- ***Did you learn a lot about an illustrator's job from* Meet Scott Nash? *What else would you like to know?***

My name is Scott Nash.
This is my wife, Nancy.

26

I make pictures for books.
This is where I work.

27

pages 26–27

First I make a sketch.
It takes a long time.

28

Then I start to paint.
This part is fun.

29

pages 28–29

This picture is done.
But I have more to do.

30

The book is done.
I hope you like it!

31

pages 30–31

Revisiting the Text

page 31

Concepts of Print

 Return Sweep; First/Last Letter in a Word

■ Call on children to sweep their hand as under the text to show how to read from left to right. Next, frame the word *book* and read it aloud. *How many letters are in this word? What is the first letter? The last letter?*

▶ Responding

Summarizing Talk with children about the steps Scott Nash goes through to illustrate a book. You may wish to point out the border art as a prompt. Ask: *Is this the way you thought Scott Nash would illustrate a book? Why do you think he sketches a picture before he paints it?*

DAY 4

 Challenge

For children who are ready for a challenge, prepare cards for the words and end marks in one or two sentences from the selection. One child builds a sentence and working with a partner, reads it in the book.

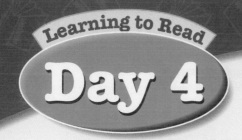

CHILDREN

- identify initial *g* for words that begin with /g/

- blend initial consonants with *-an*

MATERIALS

- ***From Apples to Zebras: A Book of ABC's,*** page 8

- **Alphafriend Cards** *Andy Apple, Gertie Goose, Pippa Pig, Vinny Volcano*

- **Letter Cards** *a, c, g, m, N, n, o, p, r, t, v*

- **Picture Cards** *can, man, pan*

- **Phonics Center:** Theme 5, Week 2, Day 4

Teacher's Note

When writing, children may ask how to spell words from the *-an* family. Help children find the word *an* on the Word Wall and add the appropriate initial consonants.

Home Connection

Challenge children to look at home for items or for names that begin with the consonant *g*. Children can draw pictures to show what they have found.

Phonics

✓ *Blending -an Words*

▶ Connect Sounds to Letters

Review Consonants *g, v, p* Using self-stick notes, cover the words on page 8 of *From Apples to Zebras: A Book of ABC's*. Then display the page and name the pictures together. Ask what letter children expect to see first in each word and why. Uncover the words so that children can check their predictions. Repeat to review *v* and *p*.

From Apples to Zebras: A Book of ABC's, page 8

Reviewing *-an* Remind children that they have learned to build words with *-an*. Ask which vowel ("helper letter") they need to build *an*. **Which Alphafriend stands for the vowel sound /ă/?** Display Andy and have children name other words that start with /ă/. *(add, actor, and, astronaut)*

Hold up Letter Cards *a* and *n*. **Watch and listen as I build a word from the Word Wall: /ă//n/, an, /ă//n/, an.**

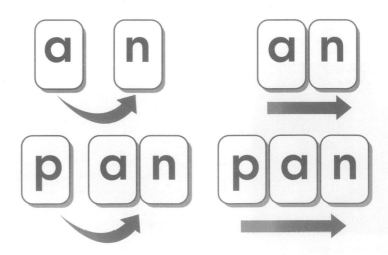

Blending *-an* Words Put Letter Card *p* in front of *an*. **Now let's blend my new word: /p//an/, pan.** Continue, having volunteers build and blend *van, can, man, Nan, ran,* and *tan.*

▶ Apply

In a pocket chart, display the Picture Card *man.* Have children say *man* with you, saying the word slowly. Help children build *man* in the pocket chart.

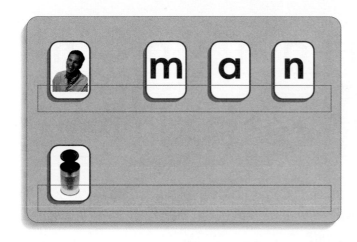

Repeat the activity to build *can* and *van.* Call on children to blend and read the words. Check and monitor children's responses.

Tell children they will build more words in the Phonics Center.

Practice Book page 151 Children will complete this page at small group time.

Phonics Library In groups today, children will also read *-an* words as they reread the **Phonics Library** story "Go, Cat!" See suggestions, page T103.

At Group Time

Phonics Center

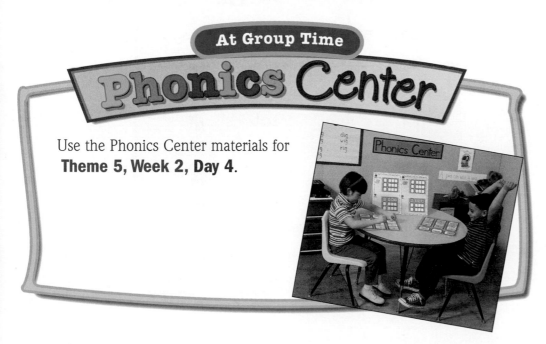

Use the Phonics Center materials for **Theme 5, Week 2, Day 4**.

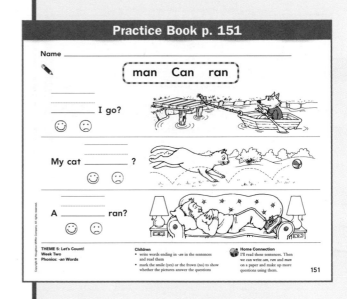

Practice Book p. 151

Diagnostic Check

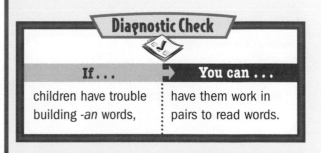

If . . .	You can . . .
children have trouble building *-an* words,	have them work in pairs to read words.

DAY 4

Phonics (T97)

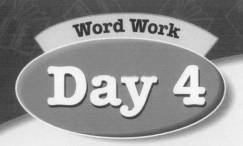
Building Words

▶ Word Families: *-at, -an*

Remind children that they have learned to build words by blending sounds together. Demonstrate by building *an* in a pocket chart, saying the sounds slowly. ***Let's build the word* pan. *Which letter should I put in front of* an?** Continue with other letters children have learned *(c, m, N, r, t, v)* to build more *-an* words.

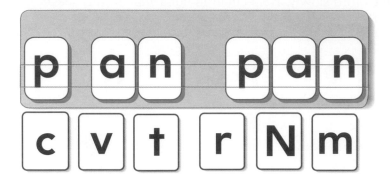

Continue, this time using Letter Cards to build *at*. ***Listen: /ă/ /t/. How many sounds do you hear? What letter spells the sound /ă/? The last sound is /t/. What letter spells that sound?***

Blend /ă/ and /t/ to read *at*. Ask which letter you should add to build *pat*. Model how to read *pat* by blending /p/ with /at/. Then replace *p* with *m*. ***What happens if I change /p/ to /m/? What word will I write?*** Continue making and blending *-at* words by substituting *c, h, b, r, s*.

Interactive Writing

 Writing a Poem

Remind children that they have been learning that words and numbers can rhyme. Display and review the charts children generated this week.

- Tell children they will now use some of their ideas to write a silly poem.

- Brainstorm topics for the poem. Use these prompts: ***What do we want our poem to be about? Should we write about a kind of pet? What pet should we write about?***

- Once a topic is chosen, use the numerals 1 to 10 to write the poem. Encourage children to participate in the writing. If a suggested word begins or ends with a known consonant, have a volunteer write it. Children can also help you build and write words that belong to the *-at* and *-an* families.

- Work with children to choose a title for the poem. Help them see that a title should tell something about the poem and catch a reader's interest.

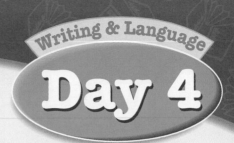
 OBJECTIVES

Children

- use rhyming words
- participate in an interactive writing activity

 Portfolio Opportunity

Save children's writing samples in their portfolios.

At Group Time

Writing Center

(**Materials** • paper • crayons or markers)

Put the chart paper from the previous activity in the Writing Center. Children "read" it on their own or with a partner. They can copy and illustrate one of the sentences. You may wish to bind pages together to form a class book.

I see 1, 1 cat plays in the sun.

I see 2, 2 cats stuck in glue.

DAY 4

Day at a Glance

Learning to Read

Revisiting the Literature:

Counting Noodles, Ten Little Puppies, Meet Scott Nash, "Go, Cat!"

☑ Phonics Review: Consonants *p, g; -at, -an Words, page T104*

Word Work

Building Words, *page T106*

Writing & Language

Independent Writing, *page T107*

 Half-Day Kindergarten

☑ Indicates lessons for tested skills. Choose additional activities as time allows.

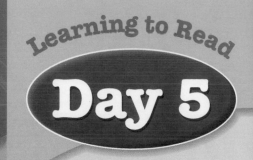

Opening

Calendar

Sunday	Monday	Tuesday	Wednesday	Thursday	Friday	Saturday
			1	2	3	4
5	6	7	8	9	10	11
12	13	14	15	16	17	18
19	20	21	22	23	24	25
26	27	28	29	30	31	

Review descriptive words you've used during your calendar routine. Make some rhyming pairs: *sunny, funny; rainy, brainy; windy, Cindy; cloudy, moudy.* Silly nonsense words are acceptable for the oral activity.

Daily Message

Interactive Writing As you write the daily message, ask volunteers to contribute words or letters they can read and write. Encourage them to spell words from the *-at* and *-an* families.

> Today we <u>can</u> look <u>at</u> our favorite books.

Word Wall

Read the Word Wall together. Then play a rhyming game: *I see a word on the wall that rhymes with* van. *The word is* an. *Raise your hand when you find a word that rhymes with* bike. *(like)*

Daily Phonemic Awareness

Blending Onset and Rime

- Display in random order the Picture Cards *log, pit, pot, vet,* and *wet.*

- *I will say some sounds to name one of the Picture Cards. You blend the sounds and raise your hand when you know which Picture Card I named: /l/ /og/.*

- When most hands are up, ask children to say the word aloud with you. *That's right! /l/ /og/, log.*

- Continue until you name all the Picture Cards.

- For children who need more practice, add these words: *vat, leg, mop, pin, pet, for, lip, nod, fan.*

Getting Ready to Learn

To help plan their day, tell children that they will

- reread and talk about all the books they've read this week.

- take home a story they can read.

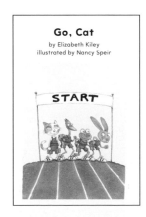

Go, Cat
by Elizabeth Kiley
illustrated by Nancy Speir

START

- write a story in their journal.

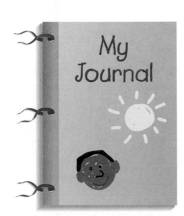

My Journal

DAY 5

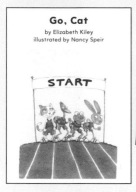

Go, Cat
by Elizabeth Kiley
illustrated by Nancy Speir

Revisiting the Literature

▶ **Literature Discussion**

Tell children that today they will compare the stories and books you shared this week: *Counting Noodles, Ten Little Puppies, Meet Scott Nash,* and "Go, Cat!" First, help children recall the selections:

■ Ask what was silly about the Read Aloud story *Counting Noodles.*

■ Review the pictures in *Ten Little Puppies*, and have children take turns telling what happened on the pages.

■ Point to photos from *Meet Scott Nash.* Select children to tell how Scott Nash illustrates a book.

■ Together, read "Go, Cat!" Ask a child to point to and read an *-an* word.

■ Ask children to vote for their favorite book of the week. Then read aloud the winning book.

✓ **Comprehension Focus:**
Story Structure: Beginning, Middle, End

Comparing Books Remind children that it's important to know what happens at the beginning, in the middle, and at the end of a story. Browse through each selection with children. After looking at each, help children develop a brief summary of the story. Encourage them to use the words *beginning, middle,* and *at the end.*

www.eduplace.com

Log on to **Education Place** for more activities relating to Let's Count!

www.bookadventure.org

This free Internet reading incentive program provides thousands of titles for children to read.

Building Fluency

▶ Rereading Familiar Texts

Phonics Library: *"Go, Cat!"* Review several of the **Phonics Library** books children have read so far. Remind them that they've learned the new word *go* this week, and that they've learned to read words with *-an*. As they reread "Go, Cat!" have children look for words with *-an*.

Review Then feature several **Phonics Library** titles in the Book Corner, and have children demonstrate their growing skills by choosing one to reread aloud. Children can alternate pages with a partner.

Oral Reading Frequent rereadings of familiar texts help children develop a less word-by-word and more expressive style in their oral reading. Model often, reading in phrases, pausing for end punctuation. Then have children try it!

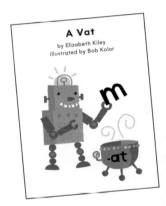

A Vat
by Elizabeth Kiley
illustrated by Bob Kolar

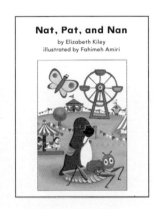

Nat, Pat, and Nan
by Elizabeth Kiley
illustrated by Fahimeh Amiri

Nat at Bat
by Elizabeth Kiley
illustrated by Holly Berry

Blackline Master 36 Children complete the page and take it home to share their reading progress.

My Reading Log

I can read

My new words

go   an

Leveled Books

The materials listed below provide reading practice for children at different levels.

Little Big Books

Reading

Ten Little Puppies
A Song from the Oral Hispanic Tradition
adapted by Elena Vázquez
illustrated by Scott Nash

Little Readers for Guided Reading

Houghton Mifflin Classroom Bookshelf

DAY 5

Home Connection

Remind children to share the take-home version of "Go, Cat!" with their families.

Day 5

Phonics Review

✔ Consonants, Word Families

OBJECTIVES

Children

- build and read words with initial consonants and short *a* + *t*, short *a* + *n*
- make sentences with high-frequency words

MATERIALS

- **Word Cards** *a, go, I, see*
- **Picture Cards** *ball, cow, up*
- **Punctuation Card:** *period*

▶ **Review**

Explain to children that they'll be word builders and word readers. Have word builders stand at the board or use magnetic letters.

- ■ *First we'll build the word an. Count the sounds: / ă / / n /. I know a stands for / ă / and n stands for / n /. Let's write an.*

- ■ Add *p* in front of your letters and have word builders do the same. Ask the word readers to read *pan*.

- ■ Work with a new group. Erase the *p*, substitute *m*, and ask word readers to read *man*.

- ■ Continue until everyone builds and reads: bat, Pat, can, sat, ran, cat, Nan, hat, tan, van, rat.

High-Frequency Word Review

 I, see, my, like, a, to, and, go

▶ Review

Give each small group the Word Cards, Picture Cards, and Punctuation Card needed to make a sentence. Each child holds one card. Children stand and arrange themselves to make a sentence for others to read. Once children read the sentence, have them act it out.

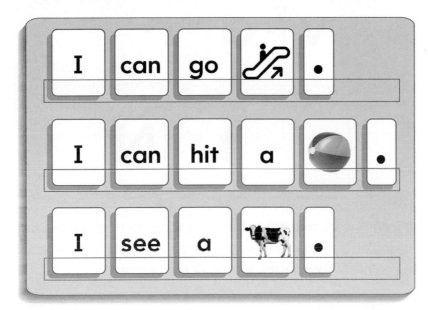

▶ Apply

Practice Book page 152 Children can complete this page independently and read it to you during small group time.

Phonics Library Have children take turns reading aloud to the class. Each child might read one page of "Go, Cat!" or a favorite **Phonics Library** selection from a previous theme. Remind readers to share the pictures.

Questions for discussion:

■ *Did you find rhyming words? Read them for us.*

■ *Find a word that starts with the same sound as Pippa Pig's name. What is the letter? What is the sound?*

■ *This week we added the word* go *to the Word Wall. Find the word* go *in "Go, Cat!"*

Practice Book p. 152

Portfolio Opportunity

Save the Practice Book page for the children's portfolios.

Diagnostic Check

If . . .	You can . . .
children need help remembering the consonant sounds,	use *From Apples to Zebras* to review consonant sounds.
children pause at high-frequency words in **Phonics Library** selections,	have partners read words on the Word Wall together.

DAY 5

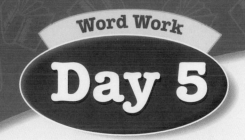

Day 5

Building Words

▶ Word Family: -an

Model how to build *an*. Along the bottom of a pocket chart, line up the letters *c, m, N, p, r, t,* and *v*. **I want to build the word van. Who can tell me what letter it should start with?** Choose a child to take the letter *v* and place it in front of *an*. Continue with *c, m, N, p, r,* and *t*. On chart paper, keep a list of all the *-an* words you make, and reread the list together.

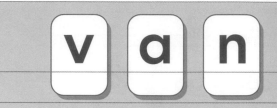

Have small groups work together to build *-an* words with magnetic letters or other alphabet blocks. Children can use their new words to create and illustrate rhyming words for the Word Bank section of their journals.

Independent Writing

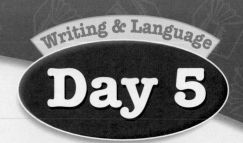
Journals Journal writing should be independent. But often children wait to be told what to write. It is often helpful to give children hints about how to think of something to write about. But assure them that they *can* choose a topic.

■ Pass out the journals. If they need it, help children generate writing ideas. *What book did you enjoy most? Can you write about it? We read a counting story. Can you write one, too? Maybe you can write about your dog. Or a dog you'd like to have.*

■ Remind children that they can use the Word Wall, along with the posted number and rhyming charts, as they write. Suggest that children can use temporary phonics spellings by saying words slowly and writing the letters they hear.

■ If time permits, allow children to share what they've written with the class.

I like my dog.

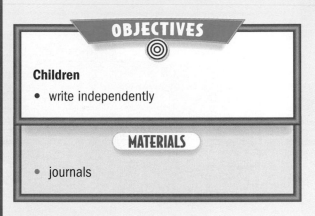

OBJECTIVES

Children
• write independently

MATERIALS

• journals

 Teacher's Note

In addition to using posted charts in the room, have children browse through *Ten Little Puppies* and *Meet Scott Nash* for writing ideas.

Portfolio Opportunity

Mark journal entries to share with children's families.

DAY 5

Literature for Week 3

Different texts for different purposes

Teacher Read Alouds:

- **Benny's Pennies**
- **Counting Noodles**
- **Peace and Quiet**

Purposes

- oral language
- listening strategy
- comprehension

Big Books:

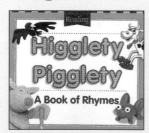

Higglety Pigglety: A Book of Rhymes

Purposes

- oral language development
- phonemic awareness

From Apples to Zebras: A Book of ABC's

Purposes

- alphabet recognition
- letters and sounds

Big Book: Main Selections

Purposes

- concepts of print
- reading strategy
- story language
- comprehension skill

Also available in Little Big Book and audiotape

Also available in Little Big Book and audiotape

Leveled Books

Art Link

Meet Scott Nash

Math Link

What's on the Menu?

31

Also in the Big Books:
- Math Link
- Art Link

Purposes
- reading strategies
- comprehension skills
- concepts of print

Phonics Library

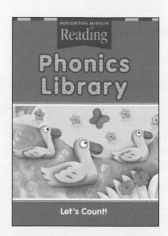

Also available in Take-Home version

Purpose
- applying phonics skills and high-frequency words

Let's Count!

On My Way Paperback

Nan Can!

by Demaris Tyler

page T153

On My Way
Practice Readers

Little Readers for Guided Reading
Collection K

Houghton Mifflin Classroom Bookshelf
Level K

Technology

www.eduplace.com
Log on to *Education Place* for more activities relating to *Let's Count!*

www.bookadventure.org
This free Internet reading incentive program provides thousands of titles for students to read.

Suggested Daily Routines

Instructional Goals

Learning to Read

- ✓ *Phonemic Awareness:* Blending Onset and Rime, Words is Oral Sentences
- *Strategy Focus:* Question, Monitor/Clarify
- ✓ *Comprehension Skill:* Story Structure: Beginning, Middle, End, Categorize and Classify
- ✓ *Phonics Skills*
- *Phonemic Awareness:* Beginning Sound /f/ Initial Consonant *F, f;* Short *a + n*
- *Compare and Review:* Initial Consonants: *g, p*
- ✓ *High-Frequency Words: and, go*
- ✓ *Concepts of Print:* Match Spoken Words to Print

Word Work

High-Frequency Word Practice: Word Families: *-an, -at*

Writing & Language

Vocabulary Skills: Using Describing Words

Writing Skills: Writing a Friendly Letter

✓ = tested skills

Leveled Books

Have children read in appropriate levels daily.

Phonics Library
On My Way Practice Readers
Little Big Books
Houghton Mifflin Classroom Bookshelf

Day 1

Opening Routines, *T114–T115*

> Word Wall

- **Phonemic Awareness:** Blending Onset and Rime, Words in Oral Sentences

Teacher Read Aloud
Peace and Quiet, T116–T119
- **Strategy:** Question
- **Comprehension:** Story Structure: Beginning, Middle, End

Phonics

Instruction
- Phonemic Awareness, Beginning Sound /f/, *T120–T121; Practice Book, 155–156*

High-Frequency Word Practice
- Words: *a, l, go, see, like, to, T122*

Oral Language
- Using Describing Words, *T123*
- Speaking, *T123*

Managing Small Groups

Teacher-Led Group
- Reread familiar **Phonics Library** selections

Independent Groups
- Finish *Practice Book, 153–156*
- Phonics Center: Theme 5, Week 3, Day 1
- Writing, Book, other Centers

Day 2

Opening Routines, *T124–T125*

> Word Wall

- **Phonemic Awareness:** Blending Onset and Rime, Words in Oral Sentences

Sharing the Big Book
Feast for 10, T126–T127
- **Strategy:** Question
- **Comprehension:** Categorize and Classify

Phonics

Instruction, Practice
- Initial Consonant *f, T128–T129*
- *Practice Book, 158*

High-Frequency Words
- Review Words: *and, go, T130–T131*
- *Practice Book, 162*

High-Frequency Word Practice
- Building Sentences, *T132*

Vocabulary Expansion
- Using Describing Words, *T133*
- Viewing and Speaking, *T133*

Managing Small Groups

Teacher-Led Group
- Begin *Practice Book, 157–159* and handwriting **Blackline Masters 162 or 188.**

Independent Groups
- Finish *Practice Book, 157–159* and handwriting **Blackline Masters 162 or 188.**
- Phonics Center: Theme 5, Week 3, Day 2
- Art, Science, other Centers

Technology

Lesson Planner CD-ROM: Customize your planning for *Let's Count!* with the Lesson Planner.

Day 3

Opening Routines, *T134–T135*

Word Wall

- **Phonemic Awareness:** Blending Onset and Rime, Words in Oral Sentences

Sharing the Big Book
Ten Little Puppies, *T136–T137*
- **Strategy:** Question
- **Comprehension:** Story Structure: Beginning, Middle, End, *T137; Practice Book,* 149
- **Concepts of Print:** Match Spoken Words to Print, *T137*

Phonics

Practice, Application
- Consonant *f,* *T138–T139*

Instruction
- Blending *-an,* *T138–T139;* *Practice Book,* 160
- **Phonics Library:** "Pat and Nan," *T139*

Building Words
- Word Family: *-an,* *T140*

✎ **Shared Writing**
- Writing a Friendly Letter, *T141*
- Speaking, *T141*

Managing Small Groups
Teacher-Led Group
- Read **Phonics Library** selection "Pat and Nan"
- Write letters *A, a;* begin **Blackline Masters 157** or **183.**
- Begin *Practice Book,* 160

Independent Groups
- Finish **Blackline Masters 157** or **183** and *Practice Book,* 160.
- Art, other Centers

Day 4

Opening Routines, *T142–T143*

Word Wall

- **Phonemic Awareness:** Blending Onset and Rime, Words in Oral Sentences

Sharing the Big Book
Math Link: "What's on the Menu?," *T144*
Art Link: "Meet Scott Nash," *T145*
- **Strategy:** Monitor/Clarify
- **Comprehension:** Categorize and Classify
- **Concepts of Print:** Match Spoken Words to Print

Phonics

Practice
- Blending *-an* Words, *T146–T147; Practice Book,* 161

Building Words
- Word Families: *-an, -at,* *T148*

✎ **Interactive Writing**
- Using Describing Words, *T149*

Managing Small Groups
Teacher-Led Group
- Reread **Phonics Library** selection "Pat and Nan," *T139*
- Begin *Practice Book,* 151
Independent Groups
- Finish *Practice Book,* 161
- **Phonics Center:** Theme 5, Week 3, Day 4
- Art, Writing, other Centers

Day 5

Opening Routines, *T150–T151*

Word Wall

- **Phonemic Awareness:** Blending Onset and Rime, Words in Oral Sentences

Revisiting the Literature
Comprehension: Story Structure: Beginning, Middle, End, Categorize and Classify, *T152*
Building Fluency
- **On My Way Practice Reader,** "Nan Can!," *T153*

Phonics

Review
- Familiar consonants; *-an, -at,* *T154*

High-Frequency Word Review
- Words: *I, see, my, like, a, to, and, go,* *T155; Practice Book,* 162

Building Words
- Word Families: *-an, -at,* *T156*

✎ **Independent Writing**
- Journals: Recording Information, *T157*

Managing Small Groups
Teacher-Led Group
- Reread familiar **Phonics Library** selections
- Begin *Practice Book,* 162, **Blackline Master 36.**

Independent Groups
- Reread **Phonics Library** selections
- Finish *Practice Book,* 162, **Blackline Master 36.**
- Centers

Suggested Daily Routines **T111**

Setting up the Centers

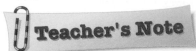

Management Tip Be sure to allow enough time for children to replace the materials they used during small group time.

Phonics Center

Materials • Phonics Center materials for Theme 5, Week 3

Pairs work together to sort Picture Cards by beginning sound and to build words using the letters *p*, *g*, and *f*, and the *-an* word family. See pages T121, T129, and T147 for this week's Phonics Center Activities.

Writing Center

Materials • paper • Picture Cards • Word Cards • "surprise can"

Children make and illustrate sentences using Picture Cards and Word Cards. Later in the week, small groups write the names of what they find in the "surprise can." See pages T122 and T149 for this week's Writing Center activities.

I see a  fox

I like to fish

Art Center

Materials • graphic organizer from Day 1 • drawing paper • water color or tempera paints • crayons or markers

Children draw and label the house from *Counting Noodles.* Children also draw an illustration of a recent gathering at their homes. After talking about pets, children draw a picture of pets they have or would like to have. Children also pretend to be Scott Nash as they illustrate a scene from *Ten Little Puppies.* See pages T123, T127, T137 and T145 for this week's Art Center activities.

Science Center

Materials • drawing paper • magazine and grocery store circulars • scissors

After rereading *Feast for 10,* children describe and sort all kinds of different foods. See page T133 for this week's Science Center activity.

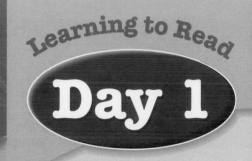

Learning to Read
Day 1

Day at a Glance

Learning to Read

Teacher Read Aloud

Peace and Quiet

☑ **Learning About / f /,** *page T120*

Word Work

High-Frequency Word Practice, *page T122*

Writing & Language

Oral Language, *page T123*

 Half-Day Kindergarten

☑ Indicates lessons for tested skills. Choose additional activities as time allows.

Opening

Calendar

Sunday	Monday	Tuesday	Wednesday	Thursday	Friday	Saturday
			1	2	3	4
5	6	7	8	9	10	11
12	13	14	15	16	17	18
19	20	21	22	23	24	25
26	27	28	29	30	31	

Use rich describing language to review the weekend's events as a preview for today's story. Encourage children to share activities that were *noisy* and those that they felt were *quiet* or *peaceful.*

Daily Message

Modeled Writing Share some of your weekend news with children. Call on volunteers to share news of their own and incorporate it into the daily message.

> I went to the movies on Saturday. Jenna and Marco saw a movie, too.

Choose a volunteer to point to and read the words *and* and *go.* **Who can read the other words in the a column?** Continue reading the remaining groups of words.

Routines

 ## Daily Phonemic Awareness
Blending Onset and Rime

As children become more adept at blending onsets and rimes, you can play this game any time you have a few minutes.

- *Listen to these word parts /f/ /at/. Say the whole word.* (fat); */p/ /in/* (pin); */l/ /ot/* (lot); */s/ /ick/* (sick).

 ## Words in Oral Sentences

- Read "Blowing Bubbles" on page 6 of *Higglety Pigglety.* **Listen: Dip your pipe and blow.** *As I say the sentence again, clap each time you hear a word. How many claps did you hear?* (five) Repeat the sentence and tally each word on chart paper. Have children count the tally marks to verify their answers.

- Continue with: *I can blow a bubble.* If children clap twice for *bubble,* explain that some words have more than one sound. Tally each word as you say the sentence again.

Getting Ready to Learn

To help plan their day, tell children that they will

- listen to a story called *Peace and Quiet.*

- meet a new Alphafriend, Fifi Fish.

- make a story map for *Peace and Quiet.*

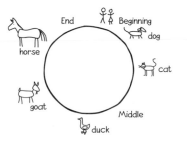

Day 1

Purposes • oral language • listening strategy • comprehension skill

Selection Summary
When household noises keep a man and a woman from sleeping, they bring animals into the house and make the situation worse. When they finally oust the animals, the original household noises bring peace and quiet to the family.

Key Concept
Things can always be worse

 English Language Learners

The onomatopoeic words in the story will not be familiar to most English language learners. As you read, imitate animal sounds and the sounds for words such as *screech* and *squeak*. Invite children to share the words for animal sounds in their native languages.

Teacher Read Aloud
Oral Language/Comprehension

▶ **Building Background**

Talk about things that might make it hard to get to sleep. Steer the discussion to noises, like those of rattling shutters, thunder, or a television. Tell children that they will listen to a story about a man and a woman who can't sleep because of noises they hear at night.

 Strategy: Question

Teacher Modeling Tell children that good readers ask questions as they read to help them understand the story.

 **Think Aloud**

Sometimes when I read a story, if I don't understand something, I'll ask a question. I'll show you how to do that as I read.

 Comprehension Focus: Story Structure: Beginning, Middle, End

Teacher Modeling Review that most stories have a beginning, middle, and an end. Often, the beginning is where you find out what the problem is.

Think Aloud

Sometimes the beginning of the story is where I can find out what the problem is. Let's read to see what happens in this story.

▶ Listening to the Story

The repetitive, cumulative nature of this story makes it one that lends itself to drama. Read it aloud and stop for children to supply familiar animal sounds. Note that the Read Aloud art is also available on the back of the Theme poster.

▶ Responding

Retelling the Story

Make a circle map to help children retell the story. Construct the map as they recall the episodes together. Children can draw the figures.

Children can use the map to retell the story. They can tell what happened in the beginning, in the middle, and at the end of the story.

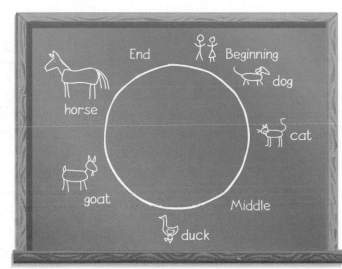

Practice Book pages 153–154 Children will complete the pages during small group time.

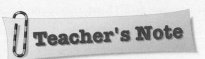

Read Aloud Tip Read the cumulative text with increasing speed and anxiety to help children sense the chaos that is taking place in the house.

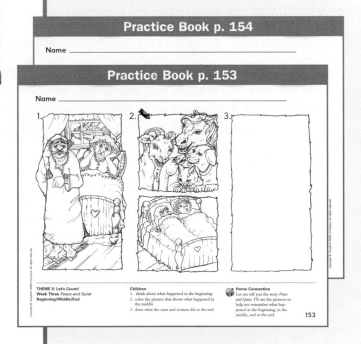

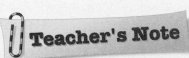

This tale is available in many familiar versions. Look for *Too Much Noise* by Ann McGovern or *Could Be Worse* by James Stevenson.

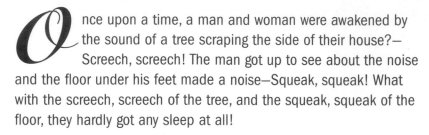

Peace and Quiet

A Russian Folktale

Once upon a time, a man and woman were awakened by the sound of a tree scraping the side of their house?—Screech, screech! The man got up to see about the noise and the floor under his feet made a noise—Squeak, squeak! What with the screech, screech of the tree, and the squeak, squeak of the floor, they hardly got any sleep at all!

In the morning, they were very tired and very cranky. "We must have peace and quiet so we can get some sleep," said the woman to her husband. "What can we do?" **(Say:** *This is the beginning of the story when we find out what the problem is. What problem did the man and woman have? If you had this problem, how would you solve it?***)**

They thought and thought and finally decided to go and ask the village elder, the wisest man in the whole country. They told the elder their problem. "Will you please help us?" they asked. "What can we do?"

After a moment, the elder asked the two if they had a dog.

"Yes," said the man, "but she's very big and she sleeps in the barn."

The elder told them to let the dog into the house. The man and woman couldn't imagine how that would help, but they were willing to try anything. But that night when they let the dog inside, things just got worse. **(Say:** *Does this make sense? Do you think it will work?***)**

The tree screeched. The floor squeaked. The dog said, "Woof, woof!"

And the man and woman got no sleep at all that night.

So they went back to the elder. "Please," they said, "We must have peace and quiet so we can get some sleep, and the dog didn't help."

Next the elder told them to get a cat. The man and woman did as they were told and went home. Now the dog chased the cat, and things got worse.

That night, the tree screeched. The floor squeaked. The dog still said, "Woof, woof!" The cat said, "Meow, meow!" And the man and woman got no sleep at all.

So again, they went back to the elder. "Please, sir," they said. "We must have peace and quiet so we can get some sleep, and the cat didn't help. What else can we do?"

"Get a duck," the elder said. When they did as they were told, the cat scratched the duck, and things got even worse.

That night, the tree screeched. The floor squeaked. The dog said, "Woof, woof!" and the cat said, "Meow, meow!" The duck said, "Quack, quack!" And the man and woman got no sleep at all. **(Say:** *In the middle of this story, we found out what the man and woman did to try to solve their problem. What did the man and woman do? Did it work? Why?***)**

This time the elder told them to get a goat. So they went home to do as they were told. Now the duck pecked the goat, and things got worse and worse.

That night, the tree screeched. The floor squeaked. The dog said, "Woof, woof!" and the cat said, "Meow, meow!" The duck said, "Quack, quack!" The goat said, "Baa, Baa!" And the man and woman got no sleep at all. **(Say:** *Time to stop and ask yourself if you understand what has happened so far. What questions do you think the end of the story will answer?***)** So the man and woman dragged themselves back to the elder one more time. And now he told them to let their horse inside. The man and woman were so tired they went home and did as they were told. Now the goat butted the horse—and things just ... got ... worse.

The man put his hands over his ears. "This can't go on! Peace and quiet," he cried. "We must have peace and quiet so we can sleep!"

Just then, the elder, curious to see if the two had followed his advice, knocked at the door. When he saw how awful things were, he said, "Now I know exactly how to solve your problem." And with that, he opened the door. He chased the horse and the goat out. He chased the duck out. And he chased the cat and the dog out.

The man and woman looked around. No more horse. No more goat. No more duck. No more cat and dog. And listen! ... NO MORE NOISE! Except ... the tree still screeched and the floor still creaked. But compared to all the noise they had before, this seemed like peace and quiet. So the man and woman both thanked the elder and then, promptly fell asleep. **(Say:** *What happened at the end of the story that tells how the man and woman got the peace and quiet they needed and why they could finally sleep?***)**

OBJECTIVES

Children

- identify pictures whose names begin with /f/

MATERIALS

- **Alphafriend Cards** Fifi Fish, Gertie Goose, Pippa Pig
- **Alphafriend Audiotape** Theme 5
- **Alphafolder** Fifi Fish
- **Picture Cards** for f, g, p
- **Phonics Center:** Theme 5, Week 3, Day 1

Home Connection

A take-home version of Fifi Fish's Song is on an **Alphafriend Blackline Master** Children can share the song with their families.

English Language Learners

Show children how to put their top teeth on their bottom lip and blow to make the sound of /f/. For Fifi Fish's song, explain that the word *fish* can name one fish or many fish.

Phonemic Awareness

✓ Beginning Sound

▶ Introducing the Alphafriend: Fifi Fish

Use the Alphafriend routine to introduce Fifi Fish.

1 **Alphafriend Riddle** Read these clues emphasizing the lfl sound:

- *This Alphafriend is an animal. Her sound is /f/. Say it with me: /f/.*

- *This animal doesn't have arms or legs. She has fins.*

- *She uses her fins to swim fast in the water.*

When most hands are up, call on children until they guess *fish*.

2 **Pocket Chart** Display Fifi Fish in a pocket chart. Say her name, emphasizing the /f/ sound and having children echo this.

3 📼 **Alphafriend Audiotape** Play Fifi Fish's song. *Listen for words that start with /f/.*

4 **Alphafolder** Have children look at the illustration and name the /f/ pictures.

5 **Summarize**

- *What is our Alphafriend's name? What is her sound?*

- *What words in our Alphafriend's song start with /f/?*

- *Each time you look at Fifi Fish this week, remember the /f/ sound.*

Fifi Fish's Song
(tune: Five Fat Turkeys)

Find Fifi Fish in the sea.

Then count all the
    fishes you see.

Fifi and the fishes
    have some fun.

Oh, what a family!

▶ Listening for / f /

Compare and Review: / g /, / p / Display Alphafriends *Gertie Goose* and *Pippa Pig* opposite *Fifi Fish*. Review each character's sound.

Hold up Picture Cards one at a time. Tell children you'll name some pictures and they should signal "thumbs up" for each one that begins like Fifi's name. Volunteers put the card below Fifi's picture. For "thumbs down" words, volunteers put cards below the correct Alphafriends.

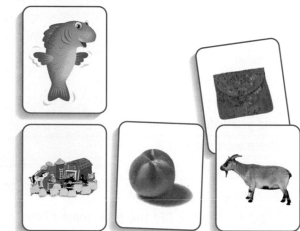

Pictures: *farm, game, peach, goat, fox, pot, girl, purse, feet, gate, fork*

Tell children they will sort more pictures in the Phonics Center today.

▶ Apply

Practice Book pages 155–156 Children will complete the pages at small group time.

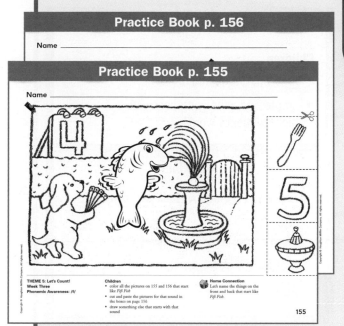

At Group Time

Phonics Center

 Use the Phonics Center materials for **Theme 5, Week 3, Day 1**.

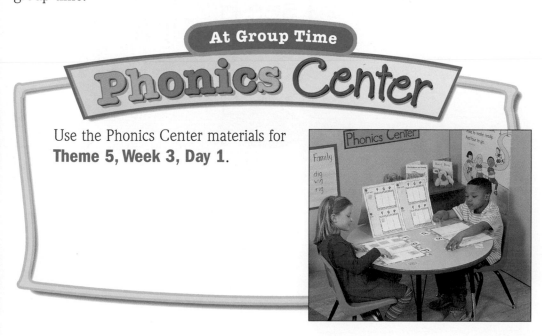

OBJECTIVES

Children

- read high-frequency words
- create and write sentences with high-frequency words

MATERIALS

- *Higglety Pigglety: A Book of Rhymes,* page 22
- **Word Cards** *a, l, go, see, like, to*
- **Picture Cards** assorted
- **Punctuation Cards:** periods

High-Frequency Word Practice

▶ Matching Words

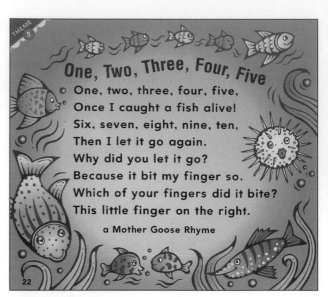

- Display Word Cards for the high-frequency words *I, a, go, to, like,* in a pocket chart. Call on children to identify each word and to match each on the Word Wall.

- Remind children that these are words they often see in books. *I'll read a poem, and you listen to hear if these words are in it.*

- Read "One, Two, Three, Four, Five" on page 22 of *Higglety Pigglety. Did you hear some of these words in the poem? Let's match the Word Cards to the words in the poem.*

Higglety Pigglety: A Book of Rhymes, page 22

✏ **Writing Opportunity** Put the Word Cards in the Writing Center. Add a few Picture Cards for children to make sentences. Suggest that they work with a partner to make a sentence. Then they can illustrate the sentence.

Oral Language

▶ Using Describing Words

Speaking Remind children that the man and the woman in *Peace and Quiet* were looking for a little peace and quiet so that they could sleep.

■ Review that describing words tell how something looks, smells, sounds, feels, or tastes. Ask children how the man and the woman describe their house. Suggest the word *noisy* if children do not.

■ Brainstorm other words to describe the house, writing the children's ideas in a graphic organizer.

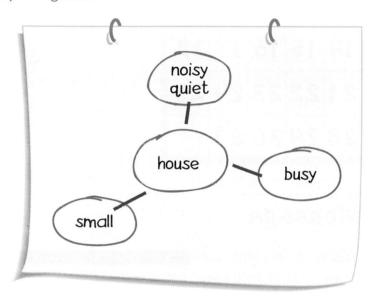

Put the graphic organizer in the Writing Center. Children can read it on their own or with a partner. First children can draw the house from the story, and then label it with their favorite describing word.

OBJECTIVES

Children
• use describing words

Portfolio Opportunity
Save children's pictures for their portfolios.

 English Language Learners

Call out the words *look, smell, sound, feel,* and *taste* and have children show you the senses they represent. Then ask children to suggest describing words that relate to the senses, such as *pretty, soft,* and *sweet.* Use realia to teach new sense words.

Day 2

Day at a Glance

Learning to Read

Big Book:

Feast for Ten

✓ **Phonics:**
Initial
Consonant *f*,
page T128

✓ **High-**
Frequency
Word Review:
and, go, *page T130*

Word Work

High-Frequency Word Practice,
page T132

Writing & Language

Vocabulary Expansion, *page T133*

 Half-Day Kindergarten

✓ Indicates lessons for tested
skills. Choose additional
activities as time allows.

Opening

Calendar

Sunday	Monday	Tuesday	Wednesday	Thursday	Friday	Saturday
			1	2	3	4
5	6	7	8	9	10	11
12	13	14	15	16	17	18
19	20	21	22	23	24	25
26	27	28	29	30	31	

Continue to use describing
language in your calendar
routine. Introduce seasonal
vocabulary: *wintry, blustery,
mild, damp.*

Daily Message

Interactive Writing As you write the
daily message, have children help you.
Ask them to supply initial and final
known consonant sounds and to help
you build and write *-an* and *-at* words.

Jake's cat ran
to the woods.

 Word Wall

Distribute Word Cards for the words on the Word Wall. Have children
match the cards to the words on the Word Wall. After a match is made, have
other children chant the spelling of the word: **a-n-d** *spells* **and; g-o** *spells* **go.**

Routines

✓ Daily Phonemic Awareness
Blending Onset and Rime

- Read "Sing a Song of Sixpence" on page 11 of *Higglety Pigglety.*

- Play a guessing game. *I'll say some sounds. You put them together to make words from the poem:* / s / / ing / (sing); / d / / ish / (dish); / k / / ing / (king); / s / / ong / (song).

- Continue with other one-syllable words: *ball, bake, six, bird.*

✓ Words in Oral Sentences

- *Clap the words as I say the sentence:* I hear the birds sing. *How many claps did you hear?* (five) As you repeat the sentence, tally each word on chart paper. Have children count the tally marks to verify their answers.

- Repeat with: *The king can eat his pie.*

Sing a Song of Sixpence

Sing a song of sixpence,
A pocket full of rye,
Four and twenty blackbirds
Baked in a pie.
When the pie was opened,
The birds began to sing.
Wasn't that a dainty dish
To set before the King?

a Mother Goose Rhyme

11

***Higglety Pigglety: A Book of Rhymes*, page 11**

Getting Ready to Learn

To help plan their day, tell children that they will

- listen to a Big Book: *Feast for Ten.*

- learn the new letters *F and f,* and see words that begin with *f.*

- name family members in the Art Center.

Learning to Read

Day 2

OBJECTIVES

Children

- categorize and classify foods
- match spoken words to print

Big Book

Purpose • concepts of print • story language
• reading strategy • comprehension skill

Extra Support

Display the chart of the food groups or the food pyramid to aid children in their discussion of the story.

Sharing the Big Book

Oral Language/Comprehension

▶ **Building Background**

Reading for Understanding You remember this book, *Feast for Ten*. This time when we read the book, see if you remember what the family makes with each food they buy.

Strategy: Question

Teacher-Student Modeling Remind children that good readers ask questions. *I want to remember who the people are who are going to have a feast. I'll keep that question in mind as I read. I can make a list of the people as I read. What do you want to keep in mind as you read the story?*

 Comprehension Focus: Categorize and Classify

Teacher-Student Modeling Review how good readers think about how to group things in a story. Look at pages 4 and 5. *A pumpkin belongs to the fruit and vegetable group. What other fruits and vegetables can you name? Chicken is a meat. What other meats can you name?*

▶ **Sharing the Story**

During the reading, make a list of the people in the story. Pause for these discussion points:

pages 12–13
Monitor/Clarify

■ *What could you do if you didn't know the meaning of the word* plump? (look at the picture; ask someone)

✓ **pages 22–23**

Concepts of Print: Match Spoken Words to Print

■ *Watch and listen. There's a word on the page for every word I say. You say it with me as I point.*

✓ **pages 28–29**

Categorize and Classify

■ *What food groups do you see? What food group is missing from the table?* (sweets) *When do you think the family will have sweets?*

▶ **Responding**

Oral Response *Who came to the feast? Tell about your favorite food made for the feast.*

Practice Book page 157 children will complete the page during group time.

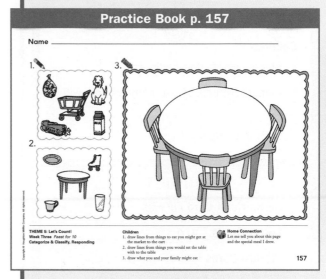

Practice Book p. 157

Name _____

THEME 5: Let's Count!
Week Three *Feast for 10*
Categorize & Classify, Responding

Children
1. draw lines from things to eat you might get at the market to the cart
2. draw lines from things you would set the table with to the table
3. draw what you and your family might eat

Home Connection
Let me tell you about this page and the special meal I drew.

157

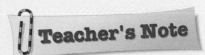

Teacher's Note

Post the list of family members from Theme 3 in the Art Center. Some children will be able to label their own family pictures using this list.

Portfolio Opportunity

Save children's pictures for their portfolios.

At Group Time

 Art Center

Materials • drawing paper • crayons or markers

Have children draw pictures of gatherings at their homes. Help children label their pictures with words that name family members.

Mom Dad Aki me.

 Challenge

MEETING INDIVIDUAL NEEDS

Have children make their own *Feast for Ten* books. Children can choose to either illustrate and write a 1 to 10 story about the shopping trip, or a 1 to 10 story about preparing for the feast.

Learning to Read
Day 2

Phonics

✓ Initial Consonant f

▶ Develop Phonemic Awareness

Beginning Sound Read aloud the lyrics from Fifi Fish's song and have children echo it line-for-line. Have them listen for the /f/ words and wiggle their "fingers" for each one they hear.

Fifi Fish's Song
(tune: Five Fat Turkeys)

Find Fifi Fish in the sea.
Then count all the
     fishes you see.
Fifi and the fishes
     have some fun.
Oh, what a family!

▶ Connect Sounds to Letters

Beginning Letter Display the Fifi Fish card, and have children name the letter on the picture. Say: *The letter* f *stands for the sound /f/, as in* fish. *When you see an* f, *remember Fifi Fish. That will help you remember the sound /f/.*

Write *fish* on the board. Underline the *f. What is the first letter in the word* fish? *(f)* Fish *starts with /f/, so* f *is the first letter I write for* fish.

Compare and Review: g, p In a pocket chart, display the Letter Cards as shown and the Picture Cards in random order. Review the sounds for *f, g,* and *p.* In turn, children can name a picture, say the beginning sound, and put the cards below the right letter.

Tell children that they will sort more pictures in the Phonics Center today.

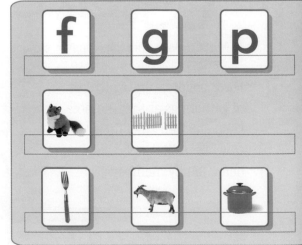

OBJECTIVES

Children

- identify words that begin with /f/
- identify pictures whose names begin with /f/
- form the letters *F, f*

MATERIALS

- **Alphafriend Card** *Fifi Fish*
- **Letter Cards** *f, g, p*
- **Picture Cards** for *f, g,* and *p*
- **Blackline Master 162**
- **Phonics Center:** Theme 5, Week 3, Day 2

 Extra Support

To help children remember the sound for *f,* point out that the letter's name gives a clue to its sound: *f,* /f/.

▶ Handwriting

Writing *F, f* Tell children that now they'll learn to write the letters that stand for / f /: capital *F* and small *f.* Write each letter as you recite the handwriting rhyme. Children can chant each rhyme as they "write" the letter in the air.

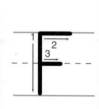

Handwriting Rhyme: F

Start at the top
and make a tall,
straight line.
Make a line to the side.
Do it one more time.

Handwriting Rhyme: f

Start at the top,
curve round and drop.
Cross the line in the
middle and then
you stop.

▶ Apply

Practice Book page 158 Children will complete this page at small group time.

Blackline Master 162 This page provides additional handwriting practice.

At Group Time

Phonics Center

Use the Phonics Center materials for **Theme 5, Week 3, Day 2**.

Name _____

THEME 5: Let's Count!
Week Three
Phonics: Initial Consonant *f*

158

Children
• write *Ff* at the top
• name the pictures *Fifi Fish* thinks about
• color and write *f* beside pictures whose names begin with the sound for *f*

Home Connection
Today we learned the letter *f.* Help me find things around the house that start with the sound for *f.*

📎 Teacher's Note

Handwriting practice for the continuous stroke style is available on **Blackline Master 188**.

Portfolio Opportunity

Save the Practice Book page to show children's grasp of the letter-sound association.

MATERIALS

- **Word Cards** *A, a, and, is, go, My, The*
- **Picture Cards** *bike, girl, green, red*
- **Punctuation Card:** period
- ***Higglety Pigglety: A Book of Rhymes,*** page 30

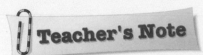 **Teacher's Note**

You will also need word cards for *van* and *can* for this lesson.

High-Frequency Words

Review Words: and, go

▶ Teach

Tell children that today they will practice reading and writing the words they learned. Say *and* and call on volunteers to use the word in context.

Write *and* on the board, and have children spell it as you point to the letters. **Spell *and* with me, a-n-d, *and.*** Then lead children in a chant, clapping on each beat, to help them remember the spelling: *a-n-d, and! a-n-d, and!*

Repeat for the word *go.*

Word Wall Have children find the words *and* and *go* on the Word Wall. Remind children to look there when they need to remember how to write the words.

▶ Practice

Reading Make word cards for *van* and *can.* Then build the following sentences in a pocket chart. Children take turns reading the sentences aloud. Leave out the pocket chart, along with additional Picture Cards, so that children can practice building and reading sentences.

Display *Higglety Pigglety: A Book of Rhymes,* page 30.

■ Share the rhyme "Stop and Go" aloud.

■ Reread the title, tracking the print. Have children point to the words *and* and *go* in the title.

■ Repeat for each line in the rhyme. If children have difficulty finding the word GO in the line *...the green means GO!* spell the word with them and compare it to the word *go* on the Word Wall. Verify that the letters spell the same word.

Practice Book p. 159

Higglety Pigglety: A Book of Rhymes, page 30

▶ Apply

Practice Book page 159 Children will read and write *and* and *go* as they complete the Practice Book page. On Day 3, they will practice reading *and* and *go* in the **Phonics Library** story "Pat and Nan."

Diagnostic Check

If . . .	You can . . .
children have problems writing or reading *and* and *go* on the Practice Book page,	have them write *and* and *go* in salt or sand.

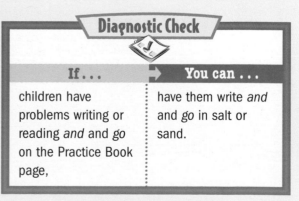

High-Frequency Word Practice

▶ Building Sentences

Tell children to think about things that go together such as, salt and pepper, bread and butter, and shoes and socks. Tell children that you want to build a sentence about a "go together."

■ Display all the Word Cards and Picture Cards in random order. Put the Word Card *I* in a pocket chart, and read it.

■ *I want the next word to be* like. *Who can find that word? That's right! This word is* like. *Now who can read my sentence so far?*

■ Continue building the sentence *I like toast and* _____. Children choose the picture card to complete the sentence and the "go together."

■ Read the sentence together.

■ Continue in a similar manner to build the following sentence: *I like red and green.*

 Writing Opportunity Have children copy a sentence from the pocket chart and illustrate it.

Vocabulary Expansion

▶ **Using Describing Words**

Remind children that describing words are words that tell how something looks, smells, sounds, feels, or tastes. Display pages 26–29 of *Feast for Ten*. Tell children that they will use some describing words to talk about the foods in the book.

Viewing and Speaking Name the foods on the page with children. Offer prompts as needed, for example: *What does fried chicken look like? What does it feel like? How does it taste?*

On chart paper, categorize children's suggestions according to the five senses.

Continue with other foods from the selection.

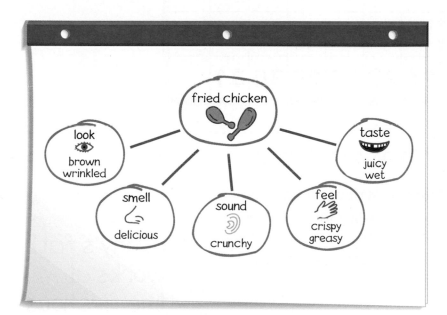

At Group Time
Science Center

Materials • magazines • drawing paper • crayons

Children can draw or cut out pictures of foods. In small groups they can describe the foods to each other. Then they can play a sorting game with the pictures. One child sorts the pictures, and the other children guess the sorting rule.

OBJECTIVES

Children
• use sensory words to describe foods

MATERIALS

• **Big Book:** *Feast for Ten*

DAY 2

English Language Learners

Teach children words to describe foods in *Feast for Ten*, such as *sweet/sour, delicious, hard/soft,* and review colors and shapes. Note that many of the foods in the story will be unfamilar to English language learners. Bring in samples for children to look at and smell if tasting is not permitted.

Day at a Glance

Learning to Read

Big Book:

Ten Little Puppies

✓ **Phonics:**
Blending f
-an, page T138

Word Work

Building Words, *page T140*

Writing & Language

Shared Writing, *page T141*

Half-Day Kindergarten

✓ Indicates lessons for tested skills. Choose additional activities as time allows.

Opening

Calendar

Sunday	Monday	Tuesday	Wednesday	Thursday	Friday	Saturday
			1	2	3	4
5	6	7	8	9	10	11
12	13	14	15	16	17	18
19	20	21	22	23	24	25
26	27	28	29	30	31	

Review the days of the week, pointing to the words as you say them. Ask volunteers to point to and name the beginning letter of each word. Then say each word together and isolate the beginning sound.

Daily Message

Modeled Writing Incorporate words that begin with *f* into the daily message. Children find and circle the *f* each time it appears.

Danny's father works at the firehouse.

Word Wall

Remind children that the words on the Word Wall are in ABC order. *I will say the alphabet, and you raise your hand when I come to a letter that begins a word on the wall. A ...are there any words that begin with a? Who will point to them and read them?*

Daily Phonemic Awareness
Blending Onset and Rime

- Read "Quack! Quack! Quack!" from *Higglety Pigglety.*

- Say: *You're going to blend some words from "Quack! Quack! Quack!" Listen:* /b/ /ig/. *Who can tell me what the word is? ...That's right,* big. *Say the sounds with me* /b/ /ig/, big.

- Continue with other words such as *duck, five, can, far, ball, lap, vet, jam, van,* and *led.*

Words in Oral Sentences

- Recall that sentences are made up of words. **Listen:** I can mop the floor. *Clap the words as I say the sentence again. How many times did you clap?*

- Continue: *I have a fan. My mom is nice. This is my dad.*

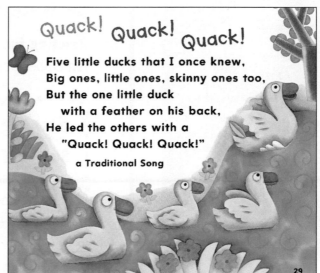

Quack! Quack! Quack!

Five little ducks that I once knew,
Big ones, little ones, skinny ones too,
But the one little duck
    with a feather on his back,
He led the others with a
    "Quack! Quack! Quack!"

a Traditional Song

29

Higglety Pigglety: A Book of Rhymes, page 29

Getting Ready to Learn

To help plan their day, tell children that they will

- reread and talk about the Big Book: *Ten Little Puppies.*

- read a story called "Pat and Nan."

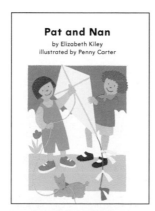

- explore pets in the Art Center.

DAY 3

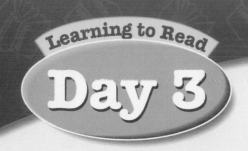

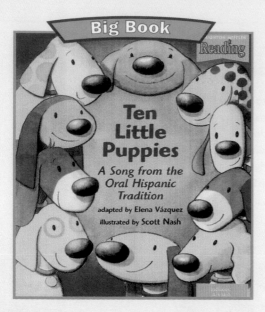

Purpose • concept of print • story language • reading strategy • skill comprehension

Sharing the Big Book
Oral Language/Comprehension

▶ **Building Background**

Reading for Understanding As we reread *Ten Little Puppies*, see if you can remember how to count backwards from ten to one.

Strategy: Question

Student Modeling Remind children that they can better remember a story by asking and answering questions that the words and pictures in the story help to answer. Ask: ***How do the pictures help you know which puppy will leave next?***

Think Aloud

One question I might ask is: How many puppies does the boy have? What questions could you ask?

 Extra Support

As you read, counters can help children keep track of how many puppies are left.

▶ Sharing the Story

As you reread the story, pause for these discussion points:

 pages 5–9

Concepts of Print: Match spoken words to print

Tell children to watch as you point and read page 5. Emphasize the three number words. Follow up with similar text on pages 7 and 9.

pages 12–13
Question

■ *Did you ask yourself what might happen to the four puppies that are left? Did you remember?*

 pages 22–23

Story Structure: Beginning, Middle, End

■ *Remember that the problem usually gets solved at the end of a story. Who can tell what happens at the end of this story?*

▶ Responding

Personal Response Have children look carefully at the humorous illustrations. Ask what they especially like and why.

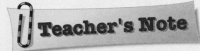

At Group Time

Art Center

Materials • drawing paper • crayons or markers

Mention that puppies and dogs are just one kind of pet people keep. Ask children to draw pictures of pets people might have or of pets they would like to have. Encourage children to label their pictures.

dog   cat   bird

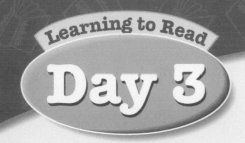

Practice Book p. 160

English Language Learners

Review the sound for /ă/. Help children blend /f/ and /an/. Remind them where to put their teeth for the /f/ sound. If possible, bring in a paper fan. Show that the word *fan* can be a naming word and action word. Use the paper fan to demonstrate the action of fanning.

Phonics

☑ *Blending f -an*

▶ Connect Sounds to Letters

Review Consonant *f* Play Fifi Fish's song, and have children clap for each /f/ word. Write *F* and *f* on the board, and list words from the song.

Blending *-an* Tell children they'll build a word with *f,* but first they'll need a vowel ("helper letter"). Display the Alphafriend *Andy Apple.* **You remember Andy Apple. Andy's letter is the vowel a, and the sound a usually stands for is /ă/. Say /ă/ with me.**

Hold up the Letter Cards *a* and *n.* Remind children that they know the sound for *n.* Model blending the sounds: /ă / /n /, *an. I've made the word* **an. The sound for a is first, and the sound for n is last.** Have volunteers move the cards as classmates blend. Monitor for accurate blending.

Word Wall Call on a volunteer to point to *an* on the Word Wall. Remind children that they can use *an* to make other words.

Blending *-an* Words Build *an* in a pocket chart. Then put *f* in front of *an,* and model blending /f / /an /, *fan.* Have children blend the sounds while you point.

Repeat with *p* to build *pan.* Then blend *-an* with other known consonants to make *can, man, Nan, ran, tan,* and *van.*

▶ Apply

Practice Book page 160 Children complete the page at small group time.

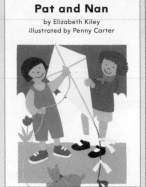

Phonics in Action

Applying Phonics Skills and High-Frequency Words

DAY 3

Purpose
- apply phonics skills
- apply high-frequency words

Pat and Nan
by Elizabeth Kiley
illustrated by Penny Carter

13

Pat sat.
Nan ran, ran, ran.

14

Nan sat.
Pat ran, ran, ran.

15

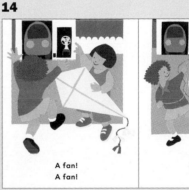

A fan!
A fan!

16

Go, !

17

Phonics/Decoding Strategy

Teacher-Student Modeling Discuss using the Strategy to read words in the **Phonics Library** story "Pat and Nan."

Think Aloud

I see the word Nan *in the title. If you didn't know that word, what would you do?* (blend /n/ and /an/ to read *Nan*) *I think that there will be someone named Nan in the story. Let's read the story to see if I'm right.*

During a picture walk, help children to predict that the story is about two friends trying to fly a kite. Use page 14 to introduce the characters Pat and Nan. On page 15, have a volunteer read *ran.* Write *ran* on the board. Then ask: **Do you see another word that is like** ran**?** (*Nan*) Choose a child to read the sentence. Then read the story with children.

▶ Coached Reading

Before reading each page aloud, have children read to themselves. These prompts will help children who need them:

page 14 *What is Pat doing? What is Nan doing? Who will read for us?*

page 16 *What did Pat and Nan find? What do you think they will use it for?*

page 17 *Pat and Nan are using the fan. What is happening to the kite?*

Home Connection

Children can color the pictures in the take-home version of "Pat and Nan." After rereading on Day 4, they can take it home to read to family members.

Phonics **T139**

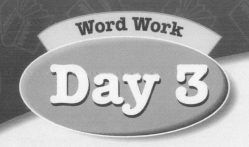

Children
- blend initial consonants with -an to read words

MATERIALS
- **Letter Cards** a, c, f, m, N, n, p, r, t, v

Building Words

▶ **Word Family: –an**

Review with children that they know all the sounds and letters to build the word *an*. Model how to build *an*, using Letter Cards. *First I'll stretch out the sounds: / ă / / n /. How many sounds are there? The first sound is / ă /. I'll put up an a to spell that. The next sound is / n /. What letter should I choose for that?*

Blend / ă / and / n / to read *an*. Then ask what letter you should add to build *fan*. Model how to read *fan* by blending / f / with / an /.

Next replace *f* with *p* and say: *What happens if I change / f / to / p /?* Continue making and blending *-an* words by substituting *c, m, N, r, t,* and *v*.

List the words on a word family chart and post it in the Writing Center. If you already have an *-an* family chart, add *fan* to it.

Have small groups work together to build *-an* words. Children can use letter tiles or other manipulatives in your collection.

Shared Writing

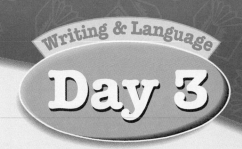
▶ Writing a Friendly Letter

Speaking Tell children that one thing families and friends do is write to one another to share news or just to say hello. Choose someone you would like to write to. It could be another kindergarten class, a child who has been sick, or the principal. Write the letter together. Guide children on the elements of a friendly letter as you write. Include a few sensory words you used earlier.

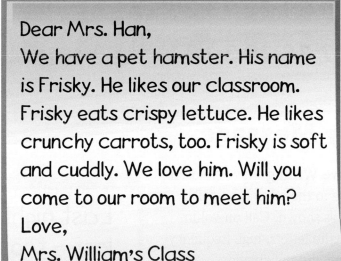

Dear Mrs. Han,
We have a pet hamster. His name is Frisky. He likes our classroom. Frisky eats crispy lettuce. He likes crunchy carrots, too. Frisky is soft and cuddly. We love him. Will you come to our room to meet him?
Love,
Mrs. William's Class

English Language Learners

Help children understand the describing words in your class letter. If possible, use real foods to demonstrate words such as *crispy* and *crunchy*. Stress word order in the sentences, *crunchy orange carrot*, for example.

DAY 3

Day 4

Day at a Glance

Learning to Read

Big Books:
What's on the Menu? Meet Scott Nash

☑ **Phonics:**
Reviewing / f /; Blending *-an* Words, *page T146*

Word Work

Building Words, *page T148*

Writing & Language

Interactive Writing, *page T149*

☀ Half-Day Kindergarten

☑ Indicates lessons for tested skills. Choose additional activities as time allows.

Opening

Calendar

Sunday	Monday	Tuesday	Wednesday	Thursday	Friday	Saturday
			1	2	3	4
5	6	7	8	9	10	11
12	13	14	15	16	17	18
19	20	21	22	23	24	25
26	27	28	29	30	31	

Find today's date on the calendar. Determine the day of the week. Count the number of Mondays there are in the month. *How many Tuesdays are there? Wednesdays?*

Daily Message

Interactive Writing Have children contribute to the text of the daily message, as shown. Call on volunteers to write letters, high-frequency words, and end punctuation.

Last night Tina lost a tooth. John can wiggle his tooth.

Have children take turns finding Word Wall words with a pointer as you call them out.

Routines

Daily Phonemic Awareness

Blending Onset and Rime

- Read "Sing a Song of Sixpence" on *Higglety Pigglety,* page 11.

- Play "Four Square Sounds" with these words from the poem: *pie, dish, king.*

Sing a Song of Sixpence

Sing a song of sixpence,
A pocket full of rye,
Four and twenty blackbirds
Baked in a pie.
When the pie was opened,
The birds began to sing.
Wasn't that a dainty dish
To set before the King?

a Mother Goose Rhyme

11

Higglety Pigglety: A Book of Rhymes, page 11

Words in Oral Sentences

- Tell children to listen as you say a sentence: **The boy had ten dogs.** *Clap the words as I say the sentence again. How many claps did you hear?*

- Repeat the sentence tallying each word on chart paper. Have children count the tally marks to verify their answers.

- Continue with: *My dog has spots. Can your dog run? We play with that dog.*

Getting Ready to Learn

To help plan their day, tell children that they will

- reread the Math Link: *What's on the Menu?* and the Art Link: *Meet Scott Nash.*

- learn to make and read new words.

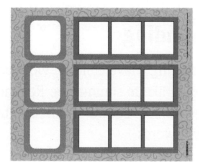

- reread a story called "Pat and Nan."

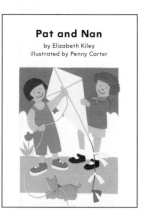

Pat and Nan
by Elizabeth Kiley
illustrated by Penny Carter

Day 4

Children

- categorize and classify items
- match spoken words to print

Big Book

What's on the Menu?

pages 32–37

Sharing the Big Books
Math Link

▶ **Building Background**

Reading for Understanding As you children reread *What's on the Menu?*, see what you remember about foods served at different places where they eat. Pause for discussion as you share the article.

> **pages 32–33**
>
> **Strategy: Monitor/Clarify**
>
> **Student Modeling** *If you were reading this for the first time and you did not know what a diner is, what would you do?*

 pages 34–35

Comprehension Focus: Categorize and Classify

How are the foods in this selection grouped?

 pages 34-35

Concepts of Print: Match spoken words to print

- *Watch and listen. There's a word on the page for every word I say. Now you say it with me as I point.*

pages 36–37

Making Judgments

- *Look at the pictures again. Do you think the foods are healthy ones? Why?*

Responding

Summarizing Have children work with partners to choose a page of the article they would like to summarize. Remind them to tell what information the page provides. Choose several children to take each illustration and tell about it in their own words.

Art Link

▶ Building Background

Reading for Understanding When you read *Meet Scott Nash* this time, have children think about how an artist takes an idea and changes it into an illustration. Pause for discussion as you share the article.

> **page 25**
>
> **Strategy: Monitor/Clarify**
>
> **Student Modeling** *When we read, we might come to something you don't understand, like the word sketch. What will you do?*

✓ **page 27**

Comprehension Focus: Categorize and Classify

Which center in the classroom is most like an artist's studio? Why?

page 31

Making Judgments

Do you think Scott Nash likes his job? Why or why not?

▶ Responding

Evaluating Encourage children to talk about what it would be like to be an artist. *Would you like to be one? Why or why not?*

At Group Time

Art Center

| **Materials** • water colors or tempera paints • paper |

Talk with children about the details and colors Scott Nash used to illustrate *Ten Little Puppies*. Then have children draw a scene from *Ten Little Puppies* or another subject they select.

Big Book

Meet Scott Nash

Ten Little Puppies
A Song from the Oral Hispanic Tradition
adapted by Elena Vásquez
Illustrated by Scott Nash

pages 25–31

Teacher's Note

Make a sign for the Art Center: ARTISTS AT WORK or STUDIO: ARTISTS WORKING.

DAY 4

MEETING INDIVIDUAL NEEDS **Challenge**

Some children may wish to use the Scott Nash piece as a model for their own auto-biographies. Children can tell about something they like to do.

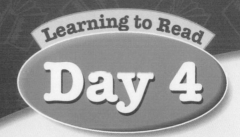

OBJECTIVES

Children

- identify initial *f* for words that begin with /f/
- blend initial consonants with *-an*

MATERIALS

- *From Apples to Zebras: A Book of ABC's*, page 7
- **Alphafriend Card** *Andy Apple*
- **Letter Cards** *a, c, f, m, N, n, p, r, t, v*
- **Picture Cards:** *can, fan, pan,*
- **Phonics Center:** Theme 5, Week 3, Day 4

Teacher's Note

During writing, children may ask how to spell words from the *-an* family. Help children find the word *an* on the Word Wall and add the appropriate initial consonant(s).

Home Connection

Challenge children to look at home for items or for names that begin with *f.* Children can draw pictures to show what they have found.

Phonics

✓ Blending *-an* Words

▶ Connect Sounds to Letters

Review Consonant *f* Cover the words on page 7 of *From Apples to Zebras: A Book of ABC's* with self-stick notes. Then display the page. Ask children to name each picture and tell what letter they expect to see first in each word and why. Have children check their predictions by removing the self-stick notes.

From Apples to Zebras: A Book of ABC's, page 7

Reviewing *-an* Review with children that in order to build a word with *f* they need a vowel ("helper letter") because every word has at least one vowel. Ask which Alphafriend stands for the vowel sound /ă/. Display Andy Apple and have children name other words that start with /ă/. *(at, address, animal, acrobat)*

Hold up Letter Cards *a* and *n.* **Watch and listen as I build a word from the Word Wall: /ă//n/, an; /ă//n/, an.**

Blending *-an* Words Put Letter Card *f* in front of *an.* **Now let's blend my new word: /f//an/, fan.** Continue, having volunteers build and blend *pan, van, can, man, Nan, ran,* and *tan.*

▶ Apply

In a pocket chart, display the Picture Card *fan*. Have children say *fan* with you, stretching out the sounds. Help children build the word *fan* in the pocket chart.

Repeat the activity to build the words *pan* and *can*. Then call on volunteers to blend and read the words. Tell children they will build more *-an* words in the Phonics Center today.

Practice Book page 161

Children will complete this page at small group time.

Phonics Library In groups today, children will also read *-an* words as they reread the **Phonics Library** story "Pat and Nan." See suggestions, page T139.

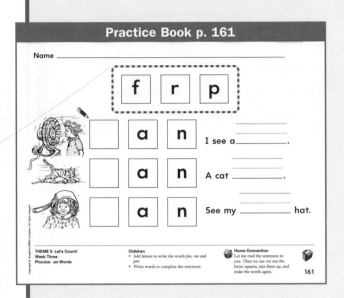

Practice Book p. 161

Use the Phonics Center materials for **Theme 5, Week 3, Day 4**.

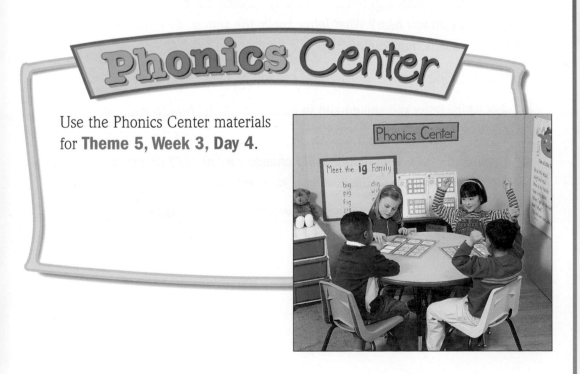

Challenge

Children who can easily build and blend *-an* words can use these words to build sentences with high-frequency words and Picture Cards.

Diagnostic Check

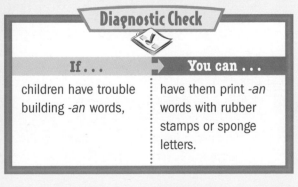

If...	You can...
children have trouble building *-an* words,	have them print *-an* words with rubber stamps or sponge letters.

DAY 4

Phonics (T147)

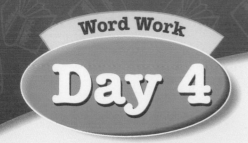

Word Work

Day 4

OBJECTIVES

Children
- build and read -an and -at words

MATERIALS

- **Letter Cards** a, b, c, h, m, N, n, p, r, s, t, v

Building Words

▶ Word Families: -an, -at

Remind children that they have learned to build words by blending sounds together. Demonstrate by stretching out the sounds for *an* as you build *an* in a pocket chart. ***Now you help me build the word* fan. *Which letter should I put in front of* an?** Use other known consonants *(c, m, N, p, r, t, v)* to replace *f* to build other *-an* words.

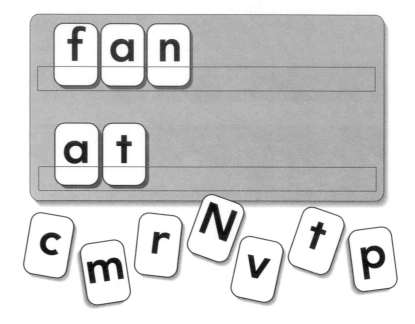

Next, use Letter Cards to build *at*. ***First I'll stretch out the sounds:* /ă/ /t/. *How many sounds do you hear? What letter spells the sound* /ă/? *The last sound is* /t/. *What letter spells that sound?*** Blend /ă/ and /t/ to read *at*.

Continue building words with initial consonants.

■ Ask which letter you should add to build *hat*. **Model how to read *hat* by blending /h/ with /at/.**

■ Replace *h* with *f*. **What happens if I change /h/ to /f/?** Continue making and blending *-at* words by substituting *b, m, p, r, s*.

Have children write some *-an* and *-at* words on white boards or paper. They can read their lists of words to a partner.

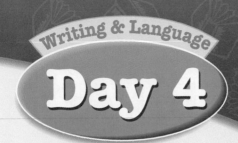

Interactive Writing

▶ Using Describing Words

Remind children that they have been working with describing words that tell how something looks, feels, smells, sounds, or tastes.

If possible, prepare a "surprise can" of items to prompt discussion. In the can you might place: a soft plush toy, some crinkly wrapping paper, a noisemaker, a bright plastic toy, and a bag of raisins. Pull out the items one at a time, generating descriptions such as soft, smooth, bright red, hard, crunchy, sticky, and loud. From these descriptions begin your interactive session. Children share the pen as they are able.

> In our Surprise Can, we found a soft toy bunny, crinkly paper, and some sticky raisins. Timmy liked the raisins best.

OBJECTIVES

Children

- use describing words in an oral context
- write letters or words for an interactive writing activity

At Group Time

Writing Center

Materials • "surprise can" • items to hide in the can • pad of paper

Have children work in small groups, selecting new items from the "surprise can" to describe. Encourage them to use what they know about letters and sounds to write the name of the "surprise" and appropriate describing words.

English Language Learners

You might have English language learners work in small groups with English speakers for the "surprise can" activity. Encourage English speakers to mime the meanings of any new describing words they use.

Day 5

Opening

Day at a Glance

Learning to Read

Revisiting the Literature:

Peace and Quiet, Feast for Ten, What's on the Menu?, Ten Little Puppies, Meet Scott Nash, "Pat and Nan"

✓ **Phonics Review: Consonants *f, g, p; -at, -an* Words,** *page T154*

Word Work

Building Words, *page T156*

Writing & Language

Independent Writing, *page T157*

 Half-Day Kindergarten

✓ Indicates lessons for tested skills. Choose additional activities as time allows.

Calendar

Sunday	Monday	Tuesday	Wednesday	Thursday	Friday	Saturday
			1	2	3	4
5	6	7	8	9	10	11
12	13	14	15	16	17	18
19	20	21	22	23	24	25
26	27	28	29	30	31	

Invite children to use sensory words to describe the day. Prompt them to tell about the sights, sounds, smells, and other sensations they experienced as they got ready for school this morning.

Daily Message

Modeled Writing After writing the message, have a child circle the letter *f* each time it appears.

Today is Ⓕriday. We need to Ⓕeed our Ⓕish, Ⓕreddy.

Distribute Word Cards for the Word Wall words. As you read the words, children holding the matching Word Cards should stand.

Daily Phonemic Awareness
Blending Onset and Rime

- Say: *I'll say some sounds. You put them together to make describing words.*
  Listen: / h / / ot / ...That's right, hot. *Say the sounds with me / h / / ot /,* hot.

- Continue the game with these describing words: *red, big, tall, new, tan.*

Words in Oral Sentences

- Remind children that sentences are made up of words. ***Listen to my sentence:***
  The ice is cold. *Clap the words as I say the sentence again. How many times did you clap?*

- Repeat the sentence and keep a tally on chart paper for each word.
  Have children count the tally marks to verify their answers.

- Repeat with the other describing words.

Getting Ready to Learn

To help plan their day, tell children that they will

- talk about all the books they've read in Let's Count!

- take home a story they can read.

- write in their journals.

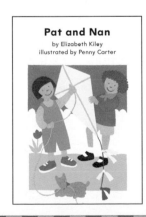

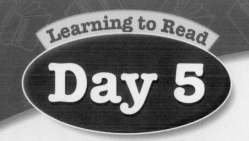

Learning to Read

Day 5

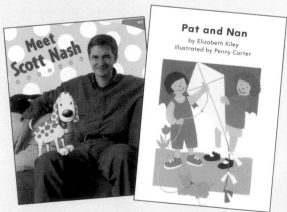

Technology

www.eduplace.con

Log on to **Education Place** for more activities relating to Let's Count!

www.bookadventure.org

This Internet reading-incentive program provides thousands of titles for children to read.

Revisiting the Literature

▶ **Literature Discussion**

Spend just a few moments on each book or article children have shared this week: *Peace and Quiet, Feast for Ten, Ten Little Puppies, What's on the Menu?, Meet Scott Nash,* and "Pat and Nan." Display the books one at a time. Help children recall each one.

- Ask: *Why is* Feast for Ten *a counting book?*

- Browse through the photos in *What's on the Menu?* and have children tell where they would like to eat and why.

- Page through the counting book *Ten Little Puppies.* Compare it to *Feast for Ten.* How is it the same? (It is a counting book, too.)

- Look at Scott Nash's illustrations in *Ten Little Puppies*, and then recall his biography.

- Together, read "Pat and Nan." Ask volunteers how they blended *ran*.

- Ask children to vote for their favorite book, and then read the winner aloud.

 Comprehension Focus: Story Structure

Remind children that stories have a beginning, a middle, and an end. Display the circle story map of the Read Aloud story *Peace and Quiet.* Help children use the map to retell the story, using the structure of the story to frame the retelling: *In the beginning …and then …finally.*

 Comprehension Focus: Categorize and Classify

Invite children to talk about the books you read this week. Point out that there are several categories of books: people, animals, and country. Have children determine which books fit in each category.

Nan Can!

On My Way Practice Reader

▶ Preparing to Read

Building Background Read the book title together, and have children point out Nan in the picture. Explain that the boy is Nan's older brother, Pat. Ask children who have younger brothers or sisters to tell about times when the little ones wanted to "help" them play.

▶ Guiding the Reading

Page through the story with children. Use the suggestions below to prepare them for reading on their own.

page 1: *What is Nan doing to the dog? Can you find the word* pat? *What mark is at the end of the first sentence? That means the first line is a question; maybe it's about Nan.*

page 3: *What is Nan doing now? How do the others feel about the noise she makes? Find the word* make... *Now find the words in fancy type. They tell what sound Nan makes with the pan. Let's read them together:* rat-a-tat-tat.

page 5: *What can Pat do with paper? Can you find the word* make *again? Let's count all the planes.*

page 8: *Do you think Pat likes having his sister help? Why?*

Prompting Strategies Listen and observe children as they point to the words and "whisper read." Use prompts such as these to help them apply strategies:

- *Point to the words in that line and read them. Did you say a word for each one?*

- *Say the sounds for the letters in this word.*

- *Does that make sense? Try again.*

▶ Responding

Ask children why they think Nan turned on the fan. Do they think her idea was a good one? Did Pat like the idea? What would they tell Pat to do the next time Nan wants to play with him?

Leveled Books

The materials listed below provide reading practice for children at different levels.

Little Big Books

Little Readers for Guided Reading

Houghton Mifflin Classroom Bookshelf

DAY 5

Children

- build and read words with initial consonants and short *a* + *t*, short *a* + *n*
- make sentences with high-frequency words

MATERIALS

- **Word Cards** *a, and, go, I, like, my, see, to*
- **Picture Cards:** *cat, dog, zoo;* assorted others
- **Punctuation Cards:** period, question mark

Phonics Review

✔ Consonants, Word Families

▶ Review

Tell children that today they will take turns being word builders and word readers. Have a group of word builders stand with you at the board.

Let's build an. *First, count the sounds. I know* a *stands for* / ă / *and* n *stands for* / n /. *Let's write these letters.*

- Have children copy *an* on the board and blend the sounds.

- Add *f* in front of your letters. Children copy and ask the rest of the class (word readers) what new word they've made.

- Ask a new group to be word builders. At your direction, they erase the *f*, write *p*, and ask the word readers to say the new word.

- Continue until everyone builds a word by replacing one letter. Examples: *man, can, Nan, ran, tan, van; bat, Pat, sat, cat, fat, hat, mat, pat, rat.*

High-Frequency Word Review

 I, see, my, like, a, to, and, go

▶ Review

Give each small group the Word Cards, Picture Cards, and Punctuation Cards needed to make a sentence. Each child holds one card. Children stand and arrange themselves to make a sentence for others to read.

▶ Apply

Practice Book page 162 Children can complete this page independently and read it to you during small group time.

Phonics Library Have children take turns reading aloud to the class. Each child might read one page of "Pat and Nan" or a favorite **Phonics Library** selection from the previous theme. Remind readers to share the pictures.

Questions for discussion:

- *Find a word in "Pat and Nan" that starts with the same sound as Fifi Fish's name. What is the letter? What is the sound?*

- *This week we practiced the words* and *and* go *on the Word Wall. Find the words* and *and* go *in "Pat and Nan."*

- *Do you hear any rhyming words in either story? What letters are the same in those words?*

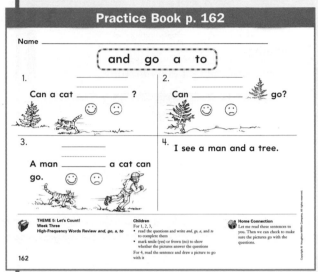

Practice Book p. 162

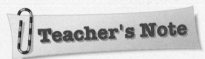

📎 Teacher's Note

You will need a word card for *Can* to build the sample sentence. You may wish to incorporate additional *-an* and *-at* words in the Review.

📦 Portfolio Opportunity

Save the Practice Book page to show children's recognition of high-frequency words.

Diagnostic Check

If . . .	▶ You can . . .
children need help remembering the consonant sounds,	have them review by matching Alphafriend Cards to Letter Cards.
children pause at high-frequency words in **Phonics Library** selections,	have partners practice reading the words on the Word Wall.

DAY 5

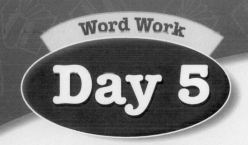

Word Work
Day 5

OBJECTIVES

Children

• build and read *-at* and *-an* words

MATERIALS

• **Letter Cards** *a, b, c, f, h, m, n, p, r, s, t, v*

Building Words

▶ ## Word Families: *-at, -an*

Model how to build *at*, stretching out the sounds. Along the bottom of a pocket chart, place the letters *b, c, f, h, m, p, r,* and *s.* **Let's build the word mat. What letter should I take from here to make mat?** Have a volunteer take the letter *m* and place it in front of *at.* Continue building *-at* words, using initial consonants *b, c, f, p, r, s,* and *t.* On chart paper, keep a list of all the *-at* words you make, and reread the list together. Examples: *at, bat, cat, fat, hat, mat, pat, rat, sat.*

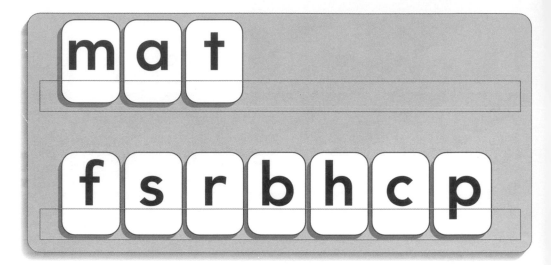

Continue the activity with *-an* words. Examples: *an, can, fan, man, pan, ran, tan, van.*

Have small groups work together to build *-at* and *-an* words with felt letters or other materials. Children can add new words to the Word Bank section of their journals and add appropriate pictures.

Independent Writing

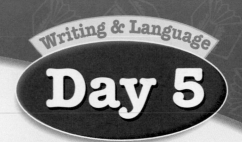
▶ Journals

Children can use journals for a variety of purposes. They can write lists, keep a record of Science Center observations, write new word lists, or write notes to you or a friend. Each week, save time for children to free-write in the journals. Use shape papers **(Blackline Master 18)** to spark writing ideas. Staple blank paper inside the fun shapes.

OBJECTIVES

Children
• write independently

MATERIALS

• journals

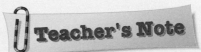

Teacher's Note

If children choose to write letters, provide them with sheets of paper to design their own stationery. Children can then copy their letters onto the stationery and "deliver" their letters to the appropriate recipients.

Portfolio Opportunity

Mark journal entries you would like to share with parents. Allow children to mark their favorite works for sharing as well.

DAY 5

English Language Learners

Have each child choose a describing word to write and draw about. Help children write the words they chose in their journals. Children can illustrate the words by drawing pictures of items that the words describe.

Theme Assessment Wrap-Up

Emerging Literacy Survey

Areas Assessed:

1. **Concepts of Print**
- Letter name knowledge
- Sound-letter association

2. **Phonemic Awareness**
- Rhyme
- Beginning sounds
- Blending onsets and rimes
- Segmenting onsets and rimes
- Blending phonemes
- Segmenting phonemes

3. **Beginning Reading and Writing**
- Word recognition
- Word writing
- Sentence dictation

 Monitoring Literacy Development

If you have administered the **Emerging Literacy Survey** as a baseline assessment of the skills children brought with them to Kindergarten, this might be a good time to re-administer all or part of it to chart progress, to identify areas of strength and need, and to test the need for early intervention.

Use the **Observation Checklist** throughout the theme to write notes indicating whether each child has a beginning, developing, or proficient understanding of reading, writing, and language concepts. (See facing page.)

▶ **Assessing Student Progress**

Formal Assessment The **Integrated Theme Test** and the **Theme Skills Test** are formal assessments used to evaluate children's performance on theme objectives.

■ The **Integrated Theme Test** assesses children's progress as readers and writers in a format that reflects instruction. Simple decodable texts test reading in context.

■ The **Theme Skills Test** assesses children's mastery of specific reading and language arts skills taught in the theme.

Observation Checklist

Name _____   Date _____

	Beginning	Developing	Proficient
Listening Comprehension • Participates in shared and choral reading			
• Listens to story attentively			
Phonemic Awareness • Can blend onsets and rimes			
• Can identify words in oral sentences			
Phonics • Can recognize initial sounds *p, g,* and *f*			
• Can build words with word family *-an*			
Concepts of Print • Distinguishes between letter, word, and sentence			
• Recognizes first/last letter in a written word			
Reading • Can read simple decodable texts			
• Can read the high-frequency words *and, go*			
Comprehension • Understands how to categorize and classify			
• Recognizes story structure: beginning, middle, end			
Writing and Language • Can write simple phrases or sentences			
• Can participate in shared and interactive writing			

For each child, write notes or checkmarks in the appropriate columns.

Theme Resources
Resources for *Let's Count!*

Contents

Hush! Little Baby

Use this music for Pippa Pig's song.

Jingle Bells

Merrily

Use this music for Gertie Goose's song.

Five Fat Turkeys

Traditional

Use this music for Fifi Fish's song.

Five Little Ducks

Use this music to accompany the Poster lyrics.

Word List

In Themes 1 through 3, the Phonics Library stories are wordless.

Theme 1

- **Phonics Skills:** none taught in this theme
- **High-Frequency Words:** none taught in this theme

Phonics Library, Week 1:
We Go to School
   wordless story

Phonics Library, Week 2:
See What We Can Do
   wordless story

Phonics Library, Week 3:
We Can Make It
   wordless story

Theme 2

- **Phonics Skills:** Initial consonants s, m, r
- **High-Frequency Words:** I, see

Phonics Library, Week 1:
My Red Boat
   wordless story
Phonics Library, Week 2:
Look at Me
   wordless story
Phonics Library, Week 3:
The Parade
   wordless story

Theme 3

- **Phonics Skills:** Initial consonants t, b, n
- **High-Frequency Words:** my, like

Phonics Library, Week 1:
The Birthday Party
   wordless story

Phonics Library, Week 2:
Baby Bear's Family
   wordless story

Phonics Library, Week 3:
Cat's Surprise
   wordless story

Theme 4

- **Phonics Skills:** Initial consonants h, v, c; words with -at
- **High-Frequency Words:** a, to

Phonics Library, Week 1:
Nat at Bat
   Words with -at: at, bat, hat, Nat, sat
   High-Frequency Words: my, see
Phonics Library, Week 2:
A Vat
   Words with -at: hat, mat, rat, vat
   High-Frequency Word: a
Phonics Library, Week 3:
Cat Sat
   Words with -at: bat, cat, hat, mat, sat
   High-Frequency Words: my, see

Theme 5

- **Phonics Skills:** Initial consonants p, g, f; words with -an
- **High-Frequency Words:** and, go

Phonics Library, Week 1:
Nat, Pat, and Nan
   Words with -an: Nan, ran
   Words with -at: Nat, Pat, sat
   High-Frequency Words: and, see
Phonics Library, Week 2:
Go, Cat!
   Words with -an: Nan, ran, Van
   Words with -at: Cat, Pat, sat
   High-Frequency Word: go
Phonics Library, Week 3:
Pat and Nan
   Words with -an: fan, Nan, ran
   Words with -at: Pat, sat
   High-Frequency Words: a, and, go

Theme 6

- **Phonics Skills:** Initial consonants l, k, qu; words with -it
- **High-Frequency Words:** is, here

Phonics Library, Week 1:
Can It Fit?
   Words with -it: fit, it, sit
   Words with -an: can, man, van
   High-Frequency Words: a, go, I, is, my
Phonics Library, Week 2:
Kit
   Words with -it: bit, fit, it, Kit, lit, sit
   Words with -an: can, pan
   Words with -at: hat
   High-Frequency Words: a, here, I
Phonics Library, Week 3:
Fan
   Words with -it: bit, quit
   Words with -an: an, Fan
   Words with -at: sat
   High-Frequency Words: a, here, is

Theme 7

- **Phonics Skills:** Initial consonants d, z; words with -ig
- **High-Frequency Words:** for, have

Phonics Library, Week 1:
Big Rig
   Words with -ig: Big, dig, Rig
   Words with -it: pit
   Words with -an: can, Dan
   High-Frequency Words: a, for
Phonics Library, Week 2:
Tan Van
   Words with -ig: Pig, Zig
   Words with -it: it
   Words with -an: can, Dan, ran, tan, van
   Words with -at: Cat, sat
   High-Frequency Words: a, have, I, is
Phonics Library, Week 3:
Zig Pig and Dan Cat
   Words with -ig: dig, Pig, Zig
   Words with -it: it
   Words with -an: can, Dan
   Words with -at: Cat, sat
   High-Frequency Words: and, for, have, here, I, is

Theme 8

▶ **Phonics Skills:** Consonant x; words with -ot, -ox

▶ **High-Frequency Words:** said, the

Phonics Library, Week 1:
Dot Got a Big Pot

Words with -ot: Dot, got, hot, lot, pot

Words with -ig: big

Words with -it: it

Words with -an: Nan

Words with -at: Nat, sat

High-Frequency Words: a, and, I, is, like, said

Phonics Library, Week 2:
The Big, Big Box

Words with -ox: box, Fox

Words with -ot: not

Words with -ig: big

Words with -it: bit, fit, hit, it

Words with -an: can, Dan, Fan

Words with -at: Cat, hat, mat, sat

High-Frequency Words: a, is, my, said, the

Phonics Library, Week 3:
A Pot for Dan Cat

Words with -ot: pot

Words with -ox: Fox

Words with -ig: big

Words with -it: fit

Words with -an: can, Dan, Fan, ran

Words with -at: Cat, sat

High-Frequency Words: a, and, see, said

Theme 9

▶ **Phonics Skills:** Initial consonants w, y; words with -et, -en

▶ **High-Frequency Words:** play, she

Phonics Library, Week 1:
Get Set! Play!

Words with -et: get, set, wet, yet

Words with -ot: got, not

Words with -ox: Fox

Words with -ig: Pig

Words with -an: can

High-Frequency Words: a, play, said

Phonics Library, Week 2:
Ben

Words with -en: Ben, Hen, men, ten

Words with -et: get, net, pet, vet, yet

Words with -ot: got, not

Words with -ox: box, Fox

Words with -it: it

Words with -an: can

High-Frequency Words: a, I, my, play, said, she, the

Phonics Library, Week 3:
Pig Can Get Wet

Words with -et: get, wet

Words with -ot: got, not

Words with -ig: big, Pig, wig

Words with -it: sit

Words with -an: can

Words with -at: Cat, sat

High-Frequency Words: a, my, play, said, she

Theme 10

▶ **Phonics Skills:** Initial consonant j; words with -ug, -ut

▶ **High-Frequency Words:** are, he

Phonics Library, Week 1:
Ken and Jen

Words with -ug: dug

Words with -en: Ken, Jen

Words with -et: wet

Words with -ot: hot

Words with -ig: big, dig

Words with -it: it, pit

High-Frequency Words: a, and, are, is

Phonics Library, Week 2:
It Can Fit

Words with -ut: but, nut

Words with -ug: jug, lug, rug

Words with -ox: box

Words with -ot: not

Words with -ig: big

Words with -it: fit, it

Words with -an: can, tan, van

Words with -at: fat, hat

High-Frequency Words: a, he, see, she

Phonics Library, Week 3:
The Bug Hut

Words with -ut: but

Words with -ug: Bug, hug, lug

Words with -ox: box

Words with -ot: Dot, got, not

Words with -ig: Big, jig

Words with -an: can, Jan

Words with -at: fat, hat

High-Frequency Words: a, here, is, she, the

Cumulative Word List

By the end of Theme 10, children will have been taught the skills necessary to read the following words.

Words with -at
at, bat, cat, fat, hat, mat, Nat, Pat, rat, sat, vat

Words with -an
an, ban, can, Dan, fan, Jan, man, Nan, pan, ran, tan, van

Words with -it
bit, fit, hit, it, kit, lit, pit, quit, sit, wit

Words with -ig
big, dig, fig, jig, pig, rig, wig, zig

Words with -ot
cot, dot, got, hot, jot, lot, not, pot, rot, tot

Words with -ox
box, fox, ox

Words with -et
bet, get, jet, let, met, net, pet, set, vet, wet, yet

Words with -en
Ben, den, hen, Jen, Ken, men, pen, ten

Words with -ug
bug, dug, hug, jug, lug, mug, rug, tug

Words with -ut
but, cut, hut, jut, nut, rut

High-Frequency Words
a, and, are, for, go, have, he, here, I, is, like, my, play, said, see, she, the, to

Technology Resources

American Melody
P. O. Box 270
Guilford, CT 06473
800-220-5557

Audio Bookshelf
174 Prescott Hill Road
Northport, ME 04849
800-234-1713

Baker & Taylor
100 Business Court Drive
Pittsburgh, PA 15205
800-775-2600

BDD Audio
1540 Broadway
New York, NY 10036
800-223-6834

Big Kids Productions
1606 Dywer Avenue
Austin, TX 78704
800-477-7811
www.bigkidsvideo.com

Blackboard Entertainment
2647 International
Boulevard
Suite 853
Oakland, CA 94601
800-968-2261
www.blackboardkids.com

Books on Tape
P. O. Box 7900
Newport Beach, CA 92658
800-626-3333

Filmic Archives
The Cinema Center
Botsford, CT 06404
800-366-1920
www.filmicarchives.com

Great White Dog Picture Company
10 Toon Lane
Lee, NH 03824
800-397-7641
www.greatwhitedog.com

HarperAudio
10 E. 53rd Street
New York, NY 10022
800-242-7737

Houghton Mifflin Company
222 Berkeley Street
Boston, MA 02116
800-225-3362

Informed Democracy
P. O. Box 67
Santa Cruz, CA 95063
831-426-3921

JEF Films
143 Hickory Hill Circle
Osterville, MA 02655
508-428-7198

Kimbo Educational
P. O. Box 477
Long Branch, NJ 07740
900-631-2187

The Learning Company (dist. for Broderbund)
1 Athenaeum Street
Cambridge, MA 02142
800-716-8506
www.learningco.com

Library Video Co.
P. O. Box 580
Wynnewood, PA 19096
800-843-3620

Listening Library
One Park Avenue
Old Greenwich, CT 06870
800-243-45047

Live Oak Media
P. O. Box 652
Pine Plains, NY 12567
800-788-1121
liveoak@taconic.net

Media Basics
Lighthouse Square
P. O. Box 449
Guilford, CT 06437
800-542-2505
www.mediabasicsvideo.com

Microsoft Corp.
One Microsoft Way
Redmond, WA 98052
800-426-9400
www.microsoft.com

National Geographic Society
1145 17th Street N. W.
Washington, D. C. 20036
800-368-2728
www.nationalgeographic.com

New Kid Home Video
1364 Palisades Beach Road
Santa Monica, CA 90401
310-451-5164

Puffin Books
345 Hudson Street
New York, NY 10014
212-366-2000

Rainbow Educational Media
4540 Preslyn Drive
Raleigh, NC 27616
800-331-4047

Random House Home Video
201 E. 50th Street
New York, NY 10022
212-940-7620

Recorded Books
270 Skipjack Road
Prince Frederick, MD 20678
800-638-1304
www.recordedbooks.com

Sony Wonder
Dist. by Professional
Media Service
19122 S. Vermont Avenue
Gardena, CA 90248
800-223-7672

Spoken Arts
8 Lawn Avenue
P. O. Box 100
New Rochelle, NY 10802
800-326-4090

SRA Media
220 E. Danieldale Road
DeSoto, TX 75115
800-843-8855

Sunburst Communications
101 Castleton Street
P. O. Box 100
Pleasantville, NY 10570
800-321-7511
www.sunburst.com

SVE & Churchill Media
6677 North Northwest
Highway
Chicago, IL 60631
800-829-1900

Tom Snyder Productions
80 Coolidge Hill Road
Watertown, MA 02472
800-342-0236
www.tomsnyder.com

Troll Communications
100 Corporate Drive
Mahwah, NJ 07430
800-526-5289

Weston Woods
12 Oakwood Avenue
Norwalk, CT 06850-1318
800-243-5020
www.scholastic.com

Index

Boldface page references indicate formal strategy and skill instruction.